*~ Dedicated to my Father **Gerald William Linton** ~*

I acknowledge and appreciate my life, for all that it is, and to those that stand beside me in support of it.

I forgive others and myself, freely accepting that every human being strives to do their best with the knowledge, experience, and vigor that they possess today. I strive to accept others for who they are, and where they are in their personal growth.

Total enlightenment or perfection is a destination seen on our horizon that we conceptualize and then endeavor to progress toward, overcoming challenges and disappointments --- driven by hope.

Each moment the universe unfolds countless treasures to be admired and cherished. Have eyes wide-open to observe and experience the many miracles that surround us.

Be present in the moment, have gratitude and give freely of yourself to others, absent of expectation. Treasure each day that affords you.

C.L.

English Language Grammar Reference & Teacher's Guide

- First Edition

for

ELT, ALT, JET *and* TESOL, TEFL, ESL, ESOL Teachers

Written By: **C. Neil Linton** - MEdLead, TESOL

Author, Educator and English Language Facilitator.

Contributing Editors: **L'Shawn Howard** - M.A. (TESOL)

Miho Yatabori - (TESOL)

The Eight (8) Parts of Speech in Simple Terms

Punctuation and Writing Guide

Cultural Awareness and Sensitivity

Classroom Management Techniques

Overview of Teaching Perspectives

Lesson Planning and Presentation Skills

Setting Context, ESL Games, Warmers or Icebreakers

Blackboard Techniques

Digital Technology in the Classroom

Role-play and Dialog Suggestions

Irregular Verb Chart

English Language Pronunciation Chart

ISBN-13: 978-0-4732-0924-7

ISBN-10: 0-4732-0924-1

(LCCN) Library of Congress Catalog Card No. 00-000000

Published by CenterLine®, Auckland, New Zealand

Cover's Digital Design by: C. Neil Linton

PRINTED IN The United States of America (U.S.A.)

10 9 8 7 6 5 4 3 2 1

ACKNOWLEDGEMENTS

During the manuscript stage, this *English Language Grammar Reference & Teacher's Guide* benefited greatly from the valuable feedback received from passionate teachers, experienced English language specialists and countless ESL students from around the world, who are, or have been, studying English as a second or additional language. Any and all feedback is priceless. Those that have a passion to seek ongoing personal and professional development can only see such feedback as an opportunity for improvement.

I'd like to thank the following individuals who have given selfless support and encouragement by imparting valuable knowledge and wisdom, answering professional questions related to English language grammar or the publishing industry, all collectively and immeasurably contributing, directly or indirectly, to this comprehensive collection:

David Hopkins, English Language Instructor and Lead Teacher for Self-Learning at King Saud University, Saudi Arabia, who had inspired me toward becoming a confident professional English language teacher; **Marc Helgesen**, ESL / ELT Author, Professor at Miyagi Gakuin Women's University, Sendai, Japan and Adjunct Professor at the Teachers College, Columbia University Master of Arts (MA) Teaching English to Speakers of Other Languages (TESOL) Program – Tokyo; **David Paul**, ESL / ELT Author and President at Language Teaching Professionals; **Andrew Gibbons** (Mentor), Senior Lecturer at Auckland University of Technology (AUT), New Zealand; **Robert Murphy**, Lecturer at The University of Kitakyushu; **Chuck Sandy** and **Curtis Kelly**, ELT materials writers and teachers; **Steven Nishida**, Director at Nara Institute of Science and Technology; **Ryan Hagglund**, Adjunct Professor at Yamagata University and President / CEO of My English Schools, Yamagata, Japan; **Paul Price**, President of Nine-Point-Nine English Schools, Yamagata, Japan; **and Michael Wyatt**, Language Coordinator at Al Sharjah, Ash Shāriqah, United Arab Emirates (U.A.E.).

My gratitude also goes to: **John King**, Founding Partner & CEO at Cultural Architecture; **Dave Logan**, Faculty Member at Marshall School of Business; **Kadambari Gladding**, TV Presenter / Director / Reporter; **Deborah Sandella**, Award-winning Author, International Speaker and originator of the R.I.M. Method at The RIM Institute, and an Associate at Jack Canfield Companies; **Sharon McGloin**, President / Owner at Experiential Alternatives, and Adjunct Professor at Avila University; **Richard Lin**, Director of the MindFirst Academy, International Meta-NLP Academy, and the International MindMap Academy; **Scott Schilling**, Owner, Schilling Sales & Marketing, Inc.; **Shawn Wiesner**, Change Agent at the Wiser Group Inc.; **Celine Egan**, Co-owner at the Direct Selling Entrepreneurs Network; **Beau Henderson**, Founder & CEO of RichLife Advisors; **Geoff Nicholson**, Founder of GN-Coaching: Stress and Empowerment Experts; **Ike Parker**, Founder / Facilitator at Brooksong Center; **Miho Yatabori**, Contributing Editor; **Norry Ascroft**; **Lloyd & Christine Hollis**, Entrepreneurs; **Tanya Davis**, The University of California, San Diego; **Wayne Miller**, Teacher & Musician; **Jacob Gwynn**, Independent Creative Professional; **Janna Androutsou**, English Language Specialist, ESL Teacher and TESOL Teacher Trainer; **Dongxue** (Sammi) **Yan**, Chartered Public Accountant (C.P.A); and **Lynn Tashima**.

Special thanks to my wonderful parents **Gerald W. and Shirley A. Linton**. Also to: **Kelvyn** and **Krystal**; **Thomas**, **Carrie** and **William**; **David**, **Gavyn**, **Meegan**, and **Robson**, who have all positively touched my life.

PERSONAL ENDORSEMENTS

My sincere gratitude goes to the following gifted individuals who have personally endorsed my life's work:

Firstly, to the one-and-only **Jack Canfield**, *America's #1 Success Coach* and a best selling author of *Chicken Soup for the Soul* book series, *The Success Principals: How to get from where you are to where you want to be,* and a teacher in *'The Secret'.*

It has been Jack's indirect and personal face-to-face mentorship, which started back in October 2009, in San Diego, California, that has inspired me to actively and passionately create, believe-in, and pursue my goals.

"I have a great deal of love in my heart for you, your chosen mission, and the work you have done and are doing in the world."

Jack Canfield

"C. Neil Linton is a man with tremendous heart. His compassion for humanity has lead him to his life's work and it is apparent upon first meeting him that he is convicted in his purpose. His insatiable thirst to learn becomes your asset once you choose to work with him and he has studied with the best of the best. If you seek a successful, driven, compassionate individual, look no further."

Erin Tullius
Human Potential and Wellness Practitioner

"C. Neil Linton not only 'talks the talk' but what is more important is he 'walks the walk.' His determination to live out genuine life change has inspired me greatly. I'm grateful for his example, friendship and work."

Mike Pate

Executive Director, Transformation Ministries

"C. Neil Linton has taken the lessons of the masters and mentors and made them his own. He has a captivating way of bringing information to life, helping others to put it into action, to move forward towards their greatest potential."

Scott Schilling

Personal Trainer, Speaker, Author and Philanthropist

CONTENTS

CHAPTER TWO: PUNCTUATION GUIDE

CHAPTER THREE: WRITING GUIDE

CHAPTER FOUR: CLASSROOM MANAGEMENT

CHAPTER FIVE: TEACHING PERSPECTIVES

CHAPTER SIX: LESSON PRESENTATION

INTRODUCTION

Who might benefit from this English Language Grammar Reference & Teacher's Guide?

This English Language Grammar Reference & Teacher's Guide has been thoughtfully created drawing on the almost two-decades of knowledge and wisdom gained as an English Language Facilitator as well as a Teaching English as a Second Language Teacher Trainer.

It has been created as a comprehensive alternative to the intimidating thick and costly technical grammar books most ESL teachers accumulate. These books are often filled with linguistic academic jargon that is not easily understood, not to mention being heavy to drag around.

The book will benefit and assist potential or new ESL teachers. Those who are:

- preparing to enter an entry-level basic CELTA, TESOL or TEFL course,
- new university graduates going to their first ESL job abroad,
- a little weak in English grammar and usage and require a tool that will provide the answers needed at a moments notice,
- in need of further professional development, upgrading or refreshing their limited practical ESL teaching skills.

With an ESL teacher's needs in mind, the book has been packed with relevant, practical classroom information, examples and advice, as well as being a comprehensive resource to the grammar and usage of the English language, in simple terms. It is also lightweight and easily carried from class-to-class for easy reference. You can't afford to be without it.

What is in the English Language Grammar Reference & Teacher's Guide?

The English Language Grammar Reference & Teacher's Guide contains six chapters and an appendix of teacher resources.

Chapter One is a comprehensive outline to the grammar and usage of the eight (8) parts of speech found in the English language, in simple terms. You will find easy to understand explanations and real-life sentence examples for each concept. The examples can be modified then transferred to the blackboard, a writing-surface, or written into presentation software, for later use.

Grammar and usage of the English language is extremely complex. This English Language Grammar Reference & Teacher's Guide was never intended to be a complete dictionary of English grammar and usage, but a comprehensive sampling for quick reference. Deeper investigation into each and every concept by an ESL teacher can be researched and knowledge improved, as needed, over time.

Chapter Two is an English language punctuation guide. The guide can be used in two ways. First, the entire collection can be used as a reference to assist the ESL teacher in the correct use of punctuation. Second, the chapter can be used as a teaching tool. Each category, or a selection of categories within the chapter, can be the basis of an independent ESL lesson. Several examples have been included to enable an ESL teacher to quickly reference a concept, modify it, and then transfer the modification to the blackboard, any writing-surface, or written into presentation software, for later use.

Chapter Three is a writing guide for either the teacher or their students. It provides invaluable information and guidance to all skill levels of writers who may attempt a simple composition, a more complex academic essay, or an advanced formal article. The mechanics from preparation to completion are basically the same.

Chapter Four, classroom management, reflects the knowledge and wisdom gained by myself as a successful generalist educator, ESL facilitator, and a TESOL / TEFL Teacher Trainer. I have also researched, observed and collected additional input from other passionate ESL educators and specialists.

The key to any teacher's implementation of a successful classroom management strategy, no matter what subject or level they face, is simple:

> First, a teacher must communicate with those that have been there before. It is essential that they tap into the experienced.

> Second, take what you have heard and experiment with it. From success comes an opportunity to build from that success. From being unsuccessful comes an opportunity for personal and professional development and growth.

Third, always take the time to analyze and reflect on all aspects of your lesson, from the first thought to the lesson's completion.

Last, but not least, make the necessary adjustments. The experiences gained provide knowledge, knowledge converts into wisdom, and wisdom is power.

This chapter outlines classroom management techniques, and includes ways to identify and avoid potential problems, provides methods to inspire or motivate students, and expresses one of the most important concepts that an ESL teacher should gain knowledge on; the importance of cultural awareness and sensitivity.

Chapter Five gives a brief comprehensive overview to the main teaching perspectives or models available. There are many approaches and methods used; some are more mainstream then others. More often than not the employer, especially in an established organization, will mandate policy regarding a specific method to be used in their ESL classrooms.

Chapter Six provides relevant, practical advice in regard to ESL lesson design and its delivery. This includes, but is not limited to, the individual components generally found in an ESL lesson plan, the environment in which delivery takes place (in most cases the classroom), the physical resources and technologies that can be considered, and the interpersonal skills needed to successfully build rapport and to be credible and respected as a professional.

*H*ow to use the English Language Grammar Reference & Teacher's Guide?

This English Language Grammar Reference & Teacher's Guide has been designed as a slightly over-sized pocket reference, intended for day-to-day use, and to be carried from class-to-class by the ESL teacher.

This book has been designed and intended as a resource, to be used while creating lessons, but also used during actual real-time teaching. As students ask grammatical or composition questions, the English Language Grammar Reference & Teacher's Guide can be quickly accessed, explanations given, and examples modified from the book, and then written on a writing surface or typed into software ready to be projected for the student's viewing.

CHAPTER ONE:
ENGLISH WORDS

EIGHT (8) PARTS OF SPEECH

PART ONE — Nouns (n.)

A *noun* is a naming word used to define a *person, place,* or *object.* A *noun* can also define an *idea, emotion (state),* or a *quality.* A *noun* can be recognized within a sentence by its *naming function, form,* and *position.* In most cases a *noun* can follow a *determiner,* such as:

Articles: *a, an, the*

a **book**	an **apple**	the **people**

Numbers: *one, two, three*

one **pencil**	two **erasers**	three **dogs**

Ordinals: *first, second, third*

first **impression**	second **house**	third **person**

Quantifiers: *a few, many, most, several, each, every, some, all, any*

a few **men**	many **ships**	most **students**
several **days**	each **life**	every **hour**
some **cheese**	all my **friends**	any **children**

Possessives: *my, your, our, their, his, her, whose*

my **car**	your **office**	our **friends**
their **opinions**	his / her **happiness**	whose **ethics**

Demonstratives: *these, those, this, that*

these / those **cats**	this **umbrella**	that **character**

A *noun* can be found before and after a verb. Examples are:

The **orange** *fell* (v.) from the **tree.**   The **boy** *shut* (v.) the **door.**

A *noun* can follow either:

Time Prepositions: *at, on, during, while, ...*

I will visit my Mom *at* **Easter**.   I will go home *on* **Friday**.

I enjoy skiing *during* **winter**.   It rained *while* **John** slept.

Place Prepositions: *in, at, on, ...*

Smoking is not allowed *in* **school**.   I study Math *at* **college**.

The Giant Sequoia tree is one of the tallest trees *on* **earth**.

Most *nouns* can have **-s** or **-es** added at the end of the word to express the *plural form* of the word. Examples are:

*house / house***s**   *church / church***es**

Most *nouns* can have an apostrophe and **-s** added to them to express *ownership* or *belonging*, called *possessive nouns*. Examples are:

*the boy***'s** *bicycles*   *the farmer***'s** *cow*   *Tony***'s** *car*

When a *multi-syllable plural noun* ends in **-s (es)**, then the apostrophe is placed after **-s'**. Examples are:

*the rugby player***s'** *uniforms*   *the ladi***es'** *dresses*

However, a *one-syllable proper noun* ending in **-s** will have an apostrophe and an additional **-s** added to the word, such as:

*Jess***'s** *report*

An exception to the above are words such as in some *names* that would be generally awkward to pronounce. An example is the name Moses:

Moses' biblical stories

A *noun* for a specific *person, title, company, organization, place,* or *thing,* as well as their abbreviations, should have the first letter of each word capitalized. Examples are:

Specific names: *September, Christmas, ...*

Person: *John Lennon, Lido Anthony 'Lee' Iacocca, ...*

Title: *Mr.* or *Mrs., Chief Executive Officer, Dean of Education, ...*

Company: *Sony Corporation of America, Hudson's Bay Co., ...*

Place: *Canada* or *CAN, The United Kingdom* or *U.K., ...*

Organization: *The National Rifle Association (NRA), ...*

Thing: *Rolls-Royce Silver Shadow, The Eiffel Tower, ...*

An exception to this rule is when a trademark utilizes a lowercase letter for the first letter of any word within the title, such as:

Apple's iPhone, iPad or iPod, etc.

Some *nouns* can be formed from adjectives by adding a suffix at the end of the adjective, such as ***-ness*** or ***-ity***. Examples are:

happy - *happi**ness*** responsible - *responsibil**ity***

Some *nouns* can be formed from verbs by adding a suffix at the end of the verb, such as: ***-tion*** or ***-sion***. Examples are:

inform - *informa**tion*** admit - *admis**sion***

Additionally, some *nouns* can be formed from verbs and occasionally from adjectives by adding a suffix at the end of the verb or adjective, such as: ***-ment***. Examples are:

A noun from a verb: replace - *replace**ment*** enjoy - *enjoy**ment***

A noun from an adjective: merry - *merri**ment***

Some *abstract nouns* can be formed from the original *noun* by adding a suffix at the end of that *noun*, such as: ***-ship*** or ***-hood***. Examples are:

*neighbor**hood*** *relation**ship*** *friend**ship***

Proper Nouns

The title and / or name of a *person, place, or thing,* is usually expressed by a *proper noun* and is always capitalized. A *proper noun* can also name a *day of the week,* a *month of the year,* a *holiday* or *festival, etc.* Examples are:

Title and / or Name of a Person: *Professor Williams, Dr. Jones, ...*

Places: *The United States of America, Yokohama, Japan, ...*

Regions: *North Island* of *New Zealand, Middle East, ...*

Districts: *District of Columbia, Rochford District, ...*

Things: *Queen Mary II* (Ship), *Apollo 13, ...*

Festivals: *Cherry Blossom Festival, Maudi Graw, ...*

Territories: *Virgin Islands, Yukon, ...*

Provinces: *British Columbia, The Western Cape, ...*

States: *Washington, New York, ...*

Holidays: *Christmas, Al Hijra, ...*

Days of the Week and Months of the Year:

Monday through *Sunday* and *January* through *December*

Note: *Proper Nouns* do not name seasons: winter, spring, etc.

✖ Common Nouns ✖

A *common noun*, opposite to a *proper noun*, names *a general item* and is not capitalized, unless they are at the beginning of a sentence. Examples are:

I was able to secure a job as a **professor**.
I drove **north**, up the island for an hour.

Some examples of other *common nouns* are:

The people you can see:

baby	*boy* or *girl*	*teenager*	*grandparent*
parent	*salesclerk*	*police-officer*	*manager*

The places you can go:

house	*restaurant*	*school*	*backyard*
beach	*river*	*mountain*	*store*

The tangible things you can see:

apple	*cat*	*bathtub*	*refrigerator*
camera	*book*	*chair*	*window*

✖ Singular and Plural Nouns ✖

Most *nouns* are either *singular* or *plural*. Most *plural forms* use either **-s** or **-es** at the end of the word. Examples are:

*building / building**s***   *cat / cat**s***   *fox / fox**es***   *box / box**es***

The letter **-y** in a *singular noun form* is changed to **i + es** in most cases. Examples are:

*lad**y** / lad**ies***   *bab**y** / bab**ies***   *tr**y** / tr**ies***   *sk**y** / sk**ies***

The letter **-f** or **-fe** can change to **v + es**. Examples are:

*cal**f** / cal**ves***   *kni**fe** / kni**ves***

However, there is less consistency with the letter **-f**, such as:

hoof   *hoo**fs***   *hoo**ves***   (all acceptable)

Some *nouns* have *irregular plural forms*. Examples are:

*child / **children***   *goose / **geese***   *tooth / **teeth***   *foot / **feet***

Some *nouns* that name a *thing*, in both the *singular* and *plural form*, are spelt the same. Examples are:

sheep / sheep   *deer / deer*   *fun / fun*   *means / means*

An exception: The word *'fish'* can be said as *'fishes'* in some cases:

Many **fishes** of the sea are endangered.

Countable Nouns

Most *common nouns* can be categorized as *countable nouns*, also referred to as '*count nouns*'. These *nouns* are written in either the *singular* or *plural form:*

one ***cup*** */ twenty* ***cups*** *one* ***child*** */ twenty* ***children***

The words *'some'* and *'any'* can be used with *countable nouns:*

He's got ***some*** *apples.* Have you got ***any*** *books?*

Uncountable Nouns

An *uncountable noun*, also referred to as a '*mass noun*', cannot be *counted* and does not have a *plural form*. These types of *nouns* name a *substance* or a *concept*. Here are some examples:

air	*water*	***gas**** (substance)	*power*
electricity	*sugar*	*salt*	*rice*

***Note:** Some *nouns* that appear to be *uncountable nouns* can also be used as *countable nouns* depending on the specific word's meaning, such as:

Going to the movies with my friends was *a* ***gas****!*

An *uncountable noun* may imply more than one item, but can be *voiced* collectively:

information	*furniture*	*luggage*	*news*
money	*currency*	*scenery*	

The *indefinite articles 'a'* and *'an'* are not usually used with *uncountable nouns:*

~~***a***~~ *music* ~~***an***~~ *information*

but, you can write:

A bottle of ***water*** or ***juice*** ***A*** grain of ***salt*** or ***rice***

A piece of ***news*** or ***information***

The words *'some'* and *'any'* are used with *uncountable nouns:*

He's got ***some*** *money.* Have you got ***any*** *salt?*

The words *a 'little'* and *'much'* are used with *uncountable nouns:*

She's got *a* ***little*** *sense.* He hasn't got ***much*** *motivation.*

�֍ Collective Nouns �֍

A *collective noun* is a *'unique'* noun that reflects a *group of people, animals, objects, concepts* or *ideas*, as a single entity, such as:

People:

army	*band*	*choir*	*jury*
corporation	*crowd*	*(a) bunch*	*committee*

Animals:

flock	*colony*	*herd*	*harem*
clutch	*pride*	*tribe*	*troop*
litter	*hive*	*gaggle*	*pack*

Objects: *deck* (of cards), *crate* (of beer), …
Abstract Ideas: *universe, ghost, spirit, love,* …
Immeasurable Concepts: *education,* …

✖ Concrete Nouns ✖

A *concrete noun* names a *physical object* that can usually be experienced through the senses: *hearing, sight, smell, taste* or *touch.*

A *concrete noun* can be *proper, common, countable, uncountable,* or a *collective noun* and appear in either *singular* or *plural forms:*

the Moon	*student*	*bread*	*coin*
perfume	*police*	*road*	*staff*

✖ Abstract Nouns ✖

An *abstract noun* names a *nonphysical object* that cannot be experienced through the senses: *hearing, sight, smell, taste* or *touch.* A *concrete noun* refers to a *concept, idea, emotion, belief,* or a *state of being:*

determination	*contentment*	*enthusiasm*	*education*
childhood	*sacrifice*	*courage*	*success*
graciousness	*amazement*	*confidence*	*tolerance*
delight	*awe*	*trust*	*wisdom*
humility	*strength*	*beauty*	*fear*

✖ Possessive Nouns ✖

A *possessive noun* is used to modify a *noun*, to indicate *ownership*. This is achieved by adding an apostrophe (') to express the possession. A *possessive noun* acts as an *adjective* to show who or what the *noun* belongs to. Examples are:

Singular nouns use an apostrophe followed by **-s***:*

> John**'s** bike   Chris**'s** book
>
> Mount Fuji**'s** trees   My boss**'s** car

Plural nouns that do not end with an **-s** use an apostrophe followed by **-s** *(~'s):*

> The People**'s** Republic of Korea
>
> (The Republic belongs to the people.)

Plural nouns ending with **-s** use an apostrophe after **-s***:*

> The student**s'** exam results
>
> (The exam results belong to the students.)

When two or more *nouns* possess the same thing, use an apostrophe followed by **-s***:*

> Tom and Jerry**'s** adventures
>
> (The adventures belong to both Tom and Jerry.)

When two or more *nouns* separately posses something, then add an apostrophe to each of the *nouns* followed by **-s***:*

> the boss**'s** and secretary**'s** cars
>
> (The boss and the secretary both have a car.)

QUOTE:
"A teacher affects eternity: he can never tell where his influence stops."

Henry Adams

DETERMINERS (det.)

A *determiner*, also known as a *non-descriptive adjective* or *noun modifier*, is a small word that precedes a *noun*. The primary purpose of a *determiner* is to *mark a noun*, or to *'determine'* which *object, person,* or other *entity* the *noun* represents.

A *determiner* can describe how many of a particular *noun* there are or to what *degree*, with the use of *numbers* or *ordinals* (e.g. one book).

A *determiner* can also inform the reader if the *noun* is *definite* (specific or having no doubt) or *indefinite* (general or unknown). Use a *definite determiner* when people know exactly which *noun* or *nouns* are being referred to (see Table 1.).

Definite Article:

    the

Possessives:

    my, your, his, her, its, our, their

Possessive Nouns *(-'s):*

    John's..., the bus's wheel..., the children's books...

Demonstratives:

    this, that, these, those

Table 1. Examples of Definite Determiners

	With Countable Nouns		With Uncountable Nouns
	singular	plural	singular
Definite Article: *the*	*the* cup	*the* cups	*the* furniture
Possessives	*my* cup	*my* cups	*my* furniture
Demonstratives	*this* cup	*these* cups	*this* furniture
	that cup	*those* cups	*that* furniture
Cardinal Numbers	*one* cup	*two* or *three* cups	—

An *indefinite determiner* can be used when referring to a *noun* or *nouns* in a vague manner (see Table 2.).

Indefinite Articles:

> *a, an*

Quantifiers:

> *all, some, any, every, several, many, more, most, ...*

Table 2. Examples of Indefinite Determiners

	With Countable Nouns		With Uncountable Nouns
	singular	plural	singular
Indefinite Articles: *a, an*	*a* cup *an* apple	~ *cups** ~ *children**	~ *furniture**
Quantifiers without Comparison	—	*all* cups	*all* furniture
		some cups	*some* furniture
	any cup	*any* cups	*any* furniture
	no cup	*no* cups	*no* furniture
	another cup *each* cup *either* cup *every* cup *neither* cup *one* cup	—	—
	—	*both* cups *enough* cups *several* cups	*enough* furniture
Quantifiers with Comparison	—	*many* cups	*much* furniture
		more cups	*more* furniture
		most cups	*most* furniture
		(a) few cups	*(a) little* furniture
		fewer cups	*less* furniture
		fewest cups	*least* furniture

Note: See *Zero Articles* (*Zero Determiners*).

Determiners are organized into several classes. These classes are:

❋ Articles ❋

Articles are the most common *determiner class*. There are three *articles*. They are the words: *a, an, the.*

Indefinite Articles: 'a' and 'an'

The *articles 'a'* and *'an'* are called *indefinite articles* and are used to tag *nonspecific nouns.*

The *articles 'a'* and *'an'* precede a *singular noun* and are used to introduce something or someone not mentioned before. Examples are:

I have **a** *very good friend* that lives nearby. He lives in **a** *house* two blocks from mine.

I am **an** *English language facilitator*. I have prepared **an** *exam* for this week's lesson.

Table 3. Indefinite Articles: 'a' and 'an'

Use the article *'a'* preceding words that begin with a spoken consonant sound: b, c, d, f, g, h, j, k, l, m, n, p, q, r, s, t, v, w, [x*], y, z			Use the article *'an'* preceding words that begin with a spoken vowel sound: a, e, i, o, u	
** See Table 53. The Phonetic Alphabet for consonant, vowel sounds.**				
(b) **a** *boy*	(c) [k] **a** *cat*	(d) **a** *dog*	(a) [æ] **an** *apple*	(e) **an** *elf*
(f) **a** *fire*	(g) **a** *girl*	(h) **a** *hotel*	(I) **an** *Indian*	(x) [e] **an** *x-ray*
(j) [dʒ] **a** *jacket*	(k) **a** *kite*	(l) **a** *leg*	(u) [ʌ] **an** *umbrella*	(o) [əʊ] **an** *open* door
(m) **a** *mall*	(n) **a** *novel*	(p) **a** *pen*	(q) [k] **a** *quarter*	(r) **a** *room*
(s) **a** *storm*	(t) **a** *tragedy*	(v) **a** *violin*	(w) **a** *war*	(*x) See above (e)
(y) [j] **a** *yacht*	(z) **a** *zipper*			

There is an exception to the usage of the *article 'an'*. If the word following the *article 'an'* has a beginning letter that is pronounced with a sound opposite its most widely used form; a consonant beginning word pronounced like a vowel and a vowel beginning word pronounced like a consonant, then the pronunciation sound determines which *article* is used. Examples are:

A unit, not ~~an~~ unit. Pronounce the word unit with a beginning-letter *'y'* sound such as you-nit, so the article *'a'* is used.

A university, not ~~an~~ university. Pronounce the word university with a beginning-letter *'y'* sound, such as *you-ni-versity*, so the article *'a'* is used.

An hour, not ~~a~~ hour. Pronounce the word *hour* with a beginning-letter *'o'* as in *'our'* because of the silent *'h'*, so the article *'an'* is used.

A preceding *article* should be used according to the pronunciation sound of the specific letter being mentioned. For example, When speaking or writing about the specific letter *'e'*, the grammar written should be as follows:

When specifically speaking or writing about the letter *'e'* , then the article *'an'* is used, not the article *'a'*, such as:

An *'e'* is a vowel in the English language.

Use the article *'an'* with these letters:

an *'f'* is... an *'h'* is... an *'r'* is... an *'s'* is... an *'x'* is...

Use the article *'a'* with this letter:

a *'u'* is....

Definite Article: the

The *definite article 'the'* is used to tag something specific; an *object* or one of a number of *the same objects* that are specifically known to the person being communicated with.

The *definite article 'the'* precedes both *singular* and *plural nouns* and is used to introduce something or someone mentioned before. Examples are:

Martin Luther King Jr. (1929 – 1968) presented a historical speech. *The speech* rallied millions to take action against prejudice.

New Zealand is said to be *a* land of unbelievable beauty. *The picturesque landscapes* will take your breath away.

Table 4. Definite Article: the

Use the article *'the'* (pronounced *thuh* [ðə]) preceding words that begin with a spoken consonant sound: b, c, d, f, g, h, j, k, l, m, n, p, q, r, s, t, v, w, x, y, z	Use the article *'the'* (pronounced *thee* [ði *or* ði:]) preceding words that begin with a spoken vowel sound: a, e, i, o, u
The *cat* and ***the*** *dog* played all day.	***The*** *English* love to drink tea and eat scones.
The *boy* and ***the*** *girl* are friends.	***The*** *car* was a classic!
The *[ðə] family* invited ***the*** *[ði* or *ði:] English girl* into their home for a year. ***The*** *[ði* or *ði:] Uncle* of ***the*** *[ðə] girl* won her a stuffed animal at ***the*** *[ðə] fair.*	

There is an exception to the example above. Some words' beginning-letter is pronounced with a sound opposite to its most widely used form; a consonant beginning word is pronounced like a vowel and a vowel beginning word pronounced like a consonant. In these cases the pronunciation sound determines which phonetically pronounced *'the'* is used, for example:

> ***the [ðə]*** unit, not *the* ***[ði*** **or** ***ði:]*** unit. The article ***the [ði*** **or** ***ði:]*** normally precedes a noun that starts with a spoken vowel sound.
>
> ***the [ði:]*** xray, not *the* ***[ðə]*** xray. The article ***the [ðə]*** normally precedes a noun that starts with a spoken consonant sound.

The above exception is also used when speaking or writing about specific letters (see Indefinite Articles *'a'* and *'an'*).

General Article Rules: 'a', 'an', and 'the'

At the first mention of something (*subject or object*) the *article 'a'* or *'an'* is used. The second and subsequent mentions of the same 'something', then use the *article 'the'.* Examples are:

> I own ***a*** *car* that is very unique. ***The*** *car* has won many prizes.
>
> I love to eat ***an*** *apple* a day. ***The*** *apple* needs to be fresh.

Zero Articles (Zero Determiners)

Generally speaking, the *zero article* is where a *noun* or a *noun phrase* [where the reference is indefinite] is not preceded by the *articles a*, *an*, or *the*.

Here are some general rules for the use of *zero articles* (no article usage) preceding some *nouns*:

1. General Abstract Nouns:

   > **Love** is all you need!

   > **Compassion** will heal the world.

2. Names of Companies, People (in singular form) or their Titles:

   > **Team New Zealand** won the most prestigious yachting race, the America's Cup, at least twice.

   > **Microsoft** has lead the world with new advancements in software.

3. Names of Places* (Continents, Countries, States, Provinces, Islands, Mountains, Lakes, Rivers, Towns, Cities, Roads, Streets, Avenues, Parks, Squares, Bridges, etc.):

   > **Australia** and **New Zealand** are commonly referred to as The Land-down-under.

   > **Park Avenue** is where I live.

   > * An exception is the grouping of a particular thing:

   >> **The** United States of America. (a collection of states)

   >> **The** Great Lakes. **The** Cascade or **The** Rocky Mountains. (a collection of lakes or mountains)

4. Names of Meals (Breakfast, Lunch, Dinner), unless formal:

   > John has **breakfast** daily, after a long 5K run.

   > **Dinner** is ready!

   >> An exception: I attended **a** banquet... (formal)

5. Names of Sports or Games:

   > **Rugby** and **poker** are my favorite sport and game, as a spectator.

   > **Chess** is a game I can't watch for very long.

6. A Noun followed by a Categorizing Letter or Number:

   > I secured Rugby World Cup Tickets for **Section E: Row 31**.

   > Auckland to Tokyo, **Flight 99**, leaves from **Gate 46**.

   > I have read **page 29** of the article as you suggested.

7. Names of Diseases:

   > **Parkinson's** is a degenerative disorder of the central nervous system that impairs motor-skills, cognitive processes, and other functions.

> ***Allergic rhinitis,*** also known as ***pollinosis***, or more commonly referred to as ***hay-fever***, is an allergic inflammation of the nasal airways, which occurs when an allergen (pollen or dust) is inhaled by a person with a sensitized immune system, which triggers antibody production.

Note: Further study is required to understand the many ways in which an *article* is or is not used with *nouns.* The above is provided as an introduction only.

Demonstratives

The *determiners this, that, these,* and *those* can be used as either a *demonstrative pronoun* (see *Demonstrative Pronouns*), or a *demonstrative determiner* (when it precedes a *noun*).

Table 5. Demonstratives: Pronoun vs. Determiner

this	singular	close	pronoun	I believe ***this*** is where I live.
			determiner	I am sure ***this*** *car* is mine.
that		far	pronoun	***That*** is the book I have read.
			determiner	***That*** *watch* is the one I want.
these	plural	close	pronoun	***These*** are going to fit me.
			determiner	***These*** *pants* shrunk.
those		far	pronoun	***Those*** are fashionable outfits.
			determiner	***Those*** *jeans* are great looking.

Possessives

A *possessive determiner* is sometimes called a *possessive adjective*, or simply a *possessive*. A *possessive determiner* is used in front of a *noun* to express *possession* or *belonging*. The *possessive determiners* that are used in the English language are:

my *your* *his* *her* *its* *our* *their*

Here are examples of *possessives* used in a sentence:

This is ***my*** *car.* Is this ***your*** *coat?*

It was ***his*** *first time to bungee.* ***Her*** *exam* is tomorrow.

✺ Quantifiers ✺

A *quantifier* is a word that precedes and modifies a *noun,* to state an unknown general quantity of something, to answer the questions: *How many...,* and *How much...,* of something there is. The *quantifier* must agree with the *noun.*

Table 6. Examples of Quantifiers Used with Nouns

Quantifiers		Examples
Quantifiers used with Countable Nouns	many (of)	I do not have **many** choices.
	few (negative)	**Few** people are coming. (almost nobody)
	a few (positive)	I have **a few** cars. (not many, but enough)
	a number (of)	I own **a number of** houses.
	several	I own **several** championship dogs.
	these / those	I own **these / those** horses.
	large number of	**A large number of** people came.
	great number of	**A great number of** people survived.
	a couple of	I own **a couple of** leather jackets.
	both	We can see **both** trees from our window.
Quantifiers used with Uncountable Nouns	much (of)	I do not have **much** time left on my exam.
	little (negative)	They had **little** hope. (almost no hope)
	a little (positive)	I have **a little** money. (enough to get by)
	a bit (of)	**A bit of** honey in my tea tastes great!
	a great deal of	He is in **a great deal of** trouble.
Quantifiers used with both Countable or Uncountable Nouns	any (negative)	They do not want **any** trouble.
	any (?)	Do you want **any** help with your study?
	hardly any	**Hardly any** visitors came to the show.
	some (positive)	I have **some** free time today.
	some (?)	Yes, may I have **some** help please?
	no	I have **no** hope in world peace.
	enough	There is **enough** fuel to last a week.
	enough (?)	Have you had **enough** dinner?
	none (of)	**None of** the children were healthy.
	a lot of	**A lot of** people like to eat strawberries.
	plenty (of)	There are **plenty of** people who can.
	lots of	There are **lots of** dogs with spots.
	most (of)	**Most of** the world lacks clean water.

❀ Numbers and Ordinals ❀

A *number* and an *ordinal* is a *determiner* when it precedes a *noun*. In this position a *number* and an *ordinal* expresses the *quantity* or *sequence of a noun*:

Numbers Expressing Quantity:

one book, **two** books, **three** books, ...

Ordinals Expressing Sequence:

first base, **second** base, **third** base, ...

General Ordinals are not directly related to Numbers but function as Determiners:

next week, **last** month, **pervious** appointment, ...

There Is a Correct Way to Write Numbers

The number zero through nine (0 – 9) should be spelled-out, and figures are used for subsequent numbers. Here are some examples:

Five *days* from now I'll leave for Tokyo. Count them – **1, 2, 3, 4, 5**.

I tutor **two** boys and **three** girls each Monday after school.

There are **25** *days* until the New Year.

Note: There is debate over the correct writing of *numbers*. The most important strategy when deciding on how to use *numbers*, when writing, is to be consistent.

❀ Pre-determiners ❀

A *pre-determiner* precedes another *determiner*. This class of words includes:

Multipliers: *double, twice, two-times, ...*

Fractional Expressions: *one-third, three-quarters, one-half, ...*

Intensifiers: *quite, rather, such, ...*

QUOTE:

"Seldom was any knowledge given to keep, but to impart; the grace of this rich jewel is lost in concealment."

Bishop Hall

PART TWO — Adjectives (adj.)

An *adjective* is a word that describes, clarifies, or modifies a *noun* or *pronoun* by giving some information about the *noun*. *Adjectives* describe the *quality*, *state* or *action* that a *noun* or *pronoun* refers to. Examples are:

Size: It is a **big** house.

Shape: It's a **round** table.

Age: He's an **old** man.

Color: It's a **red** pencil.

Origin or Religion: It's a **Buddhist** temple.

Material: I like a **wooden** boat more than a fiberglass boat.

Taste: I like to eat **bitter** chocolate.

Odor: I love the smell of the **salty** sea air.

Texture: I like to play in **squishy** mud.

Sound: The classroom was filled with **faint** whispers.

Number: **Few** people reach their full potential.

Weather: It was a **clear, dry, sunny** day.

An *adjective* is also used to clarify *an opinion* or *observation* about the *noun* and its *purpose*. Examples are:

Observation or Condition: It's a **broken** chair.

Opinion: It's a **spiritual** journey.

Purpose: He's a **rugby** player. (a *noun* that acts as an *adjective*)

Some *adjectives* end with *suffixes*. Examples are:

-ble: adorable	invisible	responsible	terrible
-al: educational	gradual	legal	essential
-an: American	Mexican	urban	Christian
-ar: popular	spectacular	polar	regular
-ent: intelligent	silent	violent	excellent
-ful: harmful	powerful	thoughtful	beautiful
-ine: canine	feminine	masculine	divine
-ile: agile	docile	fertile	hostile
-ive: informative	native	talkative	active
-ous: cautious	dangerous	enormous	famous
-ic or *-ical:* athletic	energetic	scientific	magical
-ly or *-y:* lovely	lonely	guilty	hungry
-some: awesome	handsome	lonesome	wholesome
-less: priceless	careless	homeless	blameless

Note: Many *adjectives* also end with ***-ate, -ary,*** and ***-y,*** but many *nouns* and *adverbs* also end with ***-y***, also many *nouns* end with ***-ary***, and many *nouns* and *verbs* also end with ***-ate***, so it can be confusing.

Other possible adjective endings may be:

-like:	childlike	fishlike	wifelike	zombielike
-ish:	foolish	biggish	blackish	dullish
-en:	golden	debt-ridden	broken	unproven

Adjectives Before Nouns or After Verbs

An *adjective* can come before a *noun.* If a word ends in any *suffix*, such as: ***-ate, -ary,*** or ***-y***, the word can identified as an *adjective* by where the word is and what the word is doing in the sentence. If a word is placed immediately before a *noun*, especially if the word comes between an *article* (a, an, the), a *demonstrative* (this, that, these, those), a *possessive determiner* (my, your, his, her, its, our, their), or a *quantifier* (few, many, most, several, each, every, some, all, any, etc.) and a *noun*, then it's probably an *adjective.* Here are some examples:

Article: ***The*** *dirty* ***boy*** needed a bath.

The word *dirty* comes between the article ***The*** and the noun ***boy***, so the word *dirty* is an adjective.

Demonstrative: Did you see ***that*** *savvy* ***model?***

The word *savvy* comes between the demonstrative ***that*** and the noun ***model***, so the word *savvy* is an adjective.

Possessive: These are ***my*** *old* ***clothes***.

The word *old* comes between the possessive determiner ***my*** and the noun ***clothes***, so the word *old* is an adjective.

Quantifier: We have ***few*** *ordinary* ***weekends***.

The word *ordinary* comes between the quantifier ***few*** and the noun ***weekends***, so the word *ordinary* is an adjective.

An *adjective* [or a *noun* or any word that acts as a *noun* or *adjective*] that serves as a *complement to a verb* and qualifies *the direct object* is called an *objective complement.* An *objective complement* provides additional information about the *object* and is placed after the *verb* and *object.* Examples are:

subject +	***verb (verb phrase)*** +	***object*** +	***adjective***
My Mom	keeps	her kitchen	spotless
I	like	my tea	black

Not all *complements* are *adjectives*. In the example directly below, the words *intelligent, handsome, confident,* and *thin,* are *adjectives* that complement the verb, but the phrases <u>*friends for five years*</u> and <u>*my best friend*</u> are both *noun phrases* that also complement the verb.

He is **intelligent, handsome** and **confident**.   She is **thin**.

We've been <u>friends for five years</u>.   You were <u>my best friend</u>.

Here are some tips for identifying *complementing adjectives* and *noun phrases:*

1. If the *complement* is only one word, it's most likely an *adjective*.

2. If the *complements* are a list of words, those words are most likely *adjectives*.

3. If an *article* (a, an, the) or a *possessive* (my, mine, your, yours, his, her, hers, its, our, ours, their, theirs) is present, then it most likely is a *noun phrase*.

�֎ Comparative and Superlative Adjectives ✖

One-syllable Adjectives

A *one-syllable comparative* and *superlative adjective* is formed by adding **-er** for the *comparative form* and **-est** for the *superlative form*. However, some exceptions are as follows:

If a *one-syllable adjective* ends with **-e**

Comparative Form: add **-r**

Superlative Form: add **-st**

If a *one-syllable adjective* ends with a single consonant with a vowel before it:

Comparative Form: double the consonant and add **-er**

Superlative Form: double the consonant and add **-est**

Table 7. One-syllable Comparative and Superlative Adjectives

One-syllable Adjectives	Comparative Form	Superlative Form
tall	taller	tallest
short	shorter	shortest
thin	thinner	thinnest

One-syllable Adjectives Ending with *-e*	Comparative Form	Superlative Form
large	larger	largest
wise	wiser	wisest
Ending with a single consonant with a vowel before It		
big	bigger	biggest
fat	fatter	fattest

Two-syllable Adjectives

A *two-syllable comparative* and *superlative adjective* is modified by adding the word *'more'* for the *comparative form* and *'most'* for the *superlative form*. However, some exceptions are as follows:

If an *adjective* ends with *-y*

Comparative Form: change *-y* to *i + er*

Superlative Form: change *-y* to *i + est*

If a *two-syllable adjective* ends with *-le*

Comparative Form: add *-r*

Superlative Form: add *-st*

If a *two-syllable adjective* ends with *-ow*

Comparative Form: add *-er*

Superlative Form: add *-est*

Table 8. Two-syllable Comparative and Superlative Adjectives

Two-syllable Adjectives	Comparative Form	Superlative Form
famous	more famous	most famous
peaceful	more peaceful	most peaceful
Ending with *-y*		
happy	happier	happiest
lonely	lonelier	loneliest
Ending with *-le* or *-ow*		
gentle	gentler	gentlest
narrow	narrower	narrowest

Two-syllable Adjectives	Comparative Form	Superlative Form
likely	likelier more likely	likeliest most likely
polite	politer more polite	politest most polite
simple	simpler more simple	simplest most simple

Adjectives of Three or More Syllables

A *comparative* and *superlative adjective* of *three* or *more syllables*, is modified by adding the word *'more'* for the *comparative form* and *'most'* for the *superlative form*.

Table 9. Comparative and Superlative Adjectives of Three or More Syllables

Adjectives of Three or More Syllables	Comparative Form	Superlative Form
fortunate	more fortunate	most fortunate
intelligent	more intelligent	most intelligent

Irregular Adjectives

There are some *adjectives* that are *irregular*. These *adjectives* do not follow the standard rules.

Table 10. Irregular Adjectives

Irregular Adjectives	Comparative Form	Superlative Form
bad / ill / badly	worse	worst
good / well	better	best
little	less	least
many (countable)	more	most
much (uncountable)	more	most

Meaning Differences with Adjectives

Table 11. Examples of Meaning Differences with Adjectives

	Comparative	Superlative	Description
far	farther (than) farther (up)	farthest	physical distance
	further *to consider further*	furthest *furthest from the ...*	limited to the figurative, abstract senses, extent
late	later	latest	related to time or age
	latter	last	related to order
old	older	oldest	people or things of age
	elder	eldest	senior or older person

Correct Adjective Order

When several *adjectives* in a sentence are listed, there's a specific order they must be written or spoken in. Michael Swan (Practical English Usage, Oxford University Press, 1997) writes, "Unfortunately, the rules for adjective order are very complicated, and different grammars disagree about the details" (p. 8).

Although this may be true, here is the most commonly used basic order, with examples:

determiner + judgment / attitude / opinion / feeling + size / length / height + shape + age + color + origin + religion + material + purpose + noun

1. Determiner:
   - Article: *a, an, the*
   - Possessive Determiner: my, your, *his, her, its, our, their*
   - Number or Ordinal: *two, twenty, first, second, 1st, 2nd, 3rd, ...*
   - Demonstrative: *this, that, these, those, ...*

2. Judgment, Attitude, Opinion, or Feeling: *beautiful, expensive, silly, weird, boring, magnificent, serene, breathtaking, ...*

3. Size, Length, and Height: *long, huge, tiny, tall, short, ...*

4. Shape and Width: *round, circular, oblong, narrow, ...*

5. Age: *young, old, antique, ...*

6. Color: *green, purple, ...*

7. Origin or Nationality: *British, Australian, American, ...*

8. Religion: *Buddhist, Muslim, Christian, Hindu, ...*

9. Material: *cotton, gold, diamond, wooden, ...*

10. Purpose or Type (*qualifier*): *sleeping, ...* [*sleeping* bag]

Notes:

1. If *adjectives* are listed after the *'be'* verb as *complements*, and a *qualifier* is used, the *qualifier* will proceed the *noun*. Commas should be used to separate *adjectives* within the *complement* with the two final *adjectives* being separated by the conjunction *'and'*.

   My *sleeping* bag **is** warm, big, old, blue and waterproof.

2. **Caution.** The overuse of *adjectives* [also true for the overuse of *adverbs*] may overwhelm the recipient and weaken the overall effect of the communication.

QUOTE:

"To write or even speak English is not a science but an art. There are no reliable words. Whoever writes English is involved in a struggle that never lets up even for a sentence. He is struggling against vagueness, against obscurity, against the lure of the decorative adjective, against the encroachment of Latin and Greek, and, above all, against the worn-out phrases and dead metaphors with which the language is cluttered up."

George Orwell, English Novelist and Essayist (1903-1959)

PART THREE — Pronouns (pron.)

A *pronoun* is a word that substitutes a *noun* or *noun phrase*. A *pronoun* can be used as the sentence's *subject, object,* or *complement* and can also follow a *preposition*.

✻ Personal Pronouns ✻

A *personal pronoun* is used as a substitute word in place of a *person* or *people* who are being talked about.

Table 12. Personal Pronouns

Subjective:		
	singular	I, you, he, she, it and one
acts as the subject of the sentence		*I* went to the mountain. *One* has to be diligent with one's money.
	plural	you, we and they
		They go to church every Sunday.
Objective:	singular	me, you, him, her, it and one
		Can you help *me* to find the bank?
acts as the object of the verb or the preposition	prep.	This is confidential between *you* and *me*.
	plural	you, us and them
		Could you ask *them* to join *us* for lunch?
	prep.	Please take a picture of *us* with *them*.
Possessive:	mostly singular	mine, yours, his and hers
refers to		Whose key is this, *mine* or *yours*?
something owned by someone or something previously mentioned	mostly plural	yours, ours and theirs
		Our children go to school by bus, but theirs go by car.
Reflexive:	singular	himself, herself, itself, myself, oneself and yourself
refers back to the subject of the		Henry taught *himself* to drive.
clause in which they are used	plural	ourselves, themselves and yourselves
		We helped *ourselves* to dinner.

First, Second or Third-Person

First Person

When talking about yourself to another person, refer to yourself as *I, me, my, mine,* or *myself.* Examples are:

> *I* went to the park.   *not*   (your name) went to the park.
>
> David likes *me*, not her!   John gave *mine* to her.

Second Person

When talking directly to another person (physically present or by phone), with that person as the subject, you would start the conversation by mentioning that person by their name (on the first occasion [as a point of reference]) and then subsequently refer to them as *you, your, yours,* or *yourself.* Examples are:

> Jim, are *you* ready to go?   *not*   Is (their name) ready to go?
>
> Mary, are *you* hungry? *You* said *you* were, so let's go eat!

Third Person

When talking about another person who is not present, you would start the conversation by mentioning that person by their name (on the first occasion [as a point of reference]), and then subsequently refer to them as *he, him, his, himself,* or *she, her, hers, herself.* Examples are:

> *Bob* went to the zoo. *He* fed the deer and then ~~he~~ went home.

Table 13. First, Second, or Third Person Pronoun Usage

	1st, 2nd, 3rd Person	Subject	Object	Possessive det.	Possessive Pron.	Reflective
Singular	1st	I	me	my	mine	myself
	2nd	you	you	your	yours	yourself
	3rd male	he	him	his	his	himself
	3rd female	she	her	her	hers	herself
	3rd neuter	it	it	its	its	itself
	3rd generic	one	one	one's	—	oneself
Plural	1st	we	us	our	ours	ourselves
	2nd	you	you	your	yours	yourselves
	3rd	they	them	their	theirs	themselves

✖ Demonstrative Pronouns ✖

A *demonstrative pronoun* substitutes and points attention toward a specific *person, animal, place,* or *thing* that is clearly understood or has been mentioned previously. There are four common *demonstrative pronouns:*

this   that   these   those

Table 14. Demonstrative Pronouns

Singular		*this* or *that*
	subject	**This** has been a fantastic year for Warren Buffett and his team. **That** is the room you should decorate for the job fair.
	object	Would you buy **this**? The new product made **that** obsolete.
	object of the preposition	Does the tie you bought go with **this**? Kim will upgrade the new administrative software on **that** soon.
Plural		*these* or *those*
	subject	**These** are the computer geeks that have revolutionized social-media. **Those** that wanted the next model must wait another week.
	object	Will Brad complete **these** before noon? Jacob gave **those** to the carpenter.
	object of the preposition	Please read over **these** before the deadline. Maryanne can work with **those**.

QUOTE:

"Do not be surprised when those who ignore the rules of grammar also ignore the law. After all, the law is just so much grammar."

Robert Brault

A *demonstrative pronoun* may act as an *adjective* (*demonstrative determiner*) when it is used to clarify a *noun*, rather than to substitute it. For example:

Table 15. Demonstrative Pronouns Acting Like an Adjective

	Demonstrative	Examples
this	pronoun	**This** will save us from disaster.
	determiner	**This** road is a dead end.
that	pronoun	**That** is not what I asked you.
	determiner	**That** solution will work well.
these	pronoun	**Those** will confuse us all.
	determiner	**Those** suggestions are the best I've heard all week.
those	pronoun	**These** tasted so sweet.
	determiner	**These** candies are delicious.

✖ Relative Pronouns ✖

In most cases a *relative pronoun* begins a *subordinate clause* and connects that clause to another *noun* that precedes it in the same sentence. There are several main *relative pronouns* in modern English.

Table 16. Relative Pronouns

who*		Generally used only for people:
	subjective	The person **who** phoned me last weekend is my dad.
	objective	The man **who** I talked to at the hardware store is my uncle.
whom*	objective	The person **whom** I nominated as chairman is very trustworthy.
that		Can be used for people and things:
	subjective	The noisy dog **that** barked all night belongs to my neighbor.
	objective	The team **that** I cheered for this season is my favorite.
which*		Refers to things, qualities and ideas and never for people:
	subjective	This is my uncle's antique car **which** doesn't work properly.
	objective	This is my mom's mobile phone **which** I borrowed last night.
whose*		Refers to people, things, qualities, and ideas:
	possessive	I have beautiful triplets **whose** names are Peter, Paul and Mary.
whoever		whoever, whomever, whatever, whichever
		Peter will throw the ball to **whomever** is ready to catch it.

*These words can also be used as *interrogative pronouns;* see *interrogative pronouns* in the next section.

❊ Interrogative Pronouns ❊

A *interrogative pronoun* is similar to a *relative pronoun*; the difference is that it asks a question (?) and is normally the first word in that sentence. A *interrogative pronoun* represents the unknown.

Table 17. Interrogative Pronouns

who* people	subject	Q: **Who** is the greatest boxer of all time?
		A: Either *Muhammad Ali* or *Sugar Ray Lenard* is the greatest boxer of all time.
	object	Q: **Who** do you mentor?
		A: I mentor *special-needs children.*
	complement	Q: **Who** are his teachers?
		A: They are *John and Jack.*
	with a preposition	Q: **Who** were you fishing *with*?
		A: (*With*) *a coworker of my Dad's.*
whom people	object (formal)	Q: **Whom** do you know?
		A: I know *Mr. Rogers.*
	after a preposition	Q: *To* **whom** was the exam submitted?
		A: (*To*) *Professor John Woods.*
what* non-human	subject	Q: **What**'s happened here?
		A: *The pipes burst.*
	object	Q: **What** did you achieve last year?
		A: I achieved *four Olympic gold medals.*
which* people or non-human	subject	Q: **Which** is yours?
		A: *This book* is mine.
	object	Q: **Which** will the teacher mark first?
		A: The teacher will mark and return *the second-grade exams* first.
whose people possessive form	subject	Q: There are several exams yet to be turned in. **Whose** is missing?
		A: *Matthew's* exam is missing.
	object	Q: We've bought new shoes. **Whose** do you like the most?
		A: I like *hers.*

* The *suffix −ever* is sometimes used to form a compound word with some of these pronouns: *who, what, and which.* They are used to emphasize the situation or to show reflection [deeper thought]. Examples are:

> **Whoever** would want to paint their house that terrible color?

> **Whatever** did they do to make the authorities react as they did?

> I could never decide! **Whichever** will you choose?

✼ Indefinite Pronouns ✼

An *indefinite pronoun* is vague in nature and doesn't point to any particular *noun.* Most are either *singular* or *plural;* however, some *indefinite pronouns* can be *singular* in one context and *plural* in another.

Table 18. Indefinite Pronouns

Singular	*another, anybody, anyone, anything, each, either, enough, everybody, everyone, everything, less, little, much, neither*, no-one*, nobody*, nothing*, one, other, somebody, someone, something*
	I enjoyed that cake. May I have **another**? Can **anyone** direct me to the library?
Plural	*both, few or fewer, many, others, several*
	Both were equally responsible for the company's success. **Fewer** are interested in classical music in recent years.
Singular or Plural	all, any, more, most, none*, some, such

Singular or Plural	singular	There is a lot of furniture in the showroom; **some** is a real bargain.
	plural	There are many chairs in the showroom; **some** are a real bargain.

* These *indefinite pronouns* are also referred to as *negative pronouns;* see *negative pronouns* in the next section.

Negative Pronouns

A *negative pronoun* refers to a *negative noun phrase.*

Table 19. Negative Pronouns Used in the English Language

Singular	*neither*, no one, nobody, nothing*	
	people or non-human	Tom and James took the exam. ***Neither*** passed. Do you like cats or dogs? ***Neither*** *interests me!*
	people	***No one*** came forward to answer the question. ***Nobody*** showed up.
	non-human	The lions did ***nothing*** all day but sleep.
Singular or Plural	*none*	
	people or non-human	***None*** (of the furniture) is on sale. ***None*** (of them) show the slightest interest in the history of Jazz music.

****Neither*** is the negative form of ***either*** and can be used before a *noun.*

Reciprocal Pronouns

There are only two *reciprocal pronouns, 'each other'* and *'one another'.* Both of these *reciprocal pronouns* have the same meaning. They are used when two or more subjects are interacting with or have a mutual relationship with each other.

Gerald and Shirley have been married to ***each other*** for 50+ years.

Gerald and Shirley have been married to ***one another*** for 50+ years.

QUOTE:

"Try to use the pronoun 'we' instead of 'you' and speak about the intended result instead of the failed attempt."

Terri Lonier

PART FOUR — Verbs (v.)

Most *verbs* are *action verbs*, also referred to as *dynamic verbs. Verbs* are things that a person can *'do'* or ask someone else to *'do'* (play, run, talk, see, etc.), or give the idea of *'existence'* or *'state of being'* (be, exist, seem, belong, etc.), for example:

Chris ***read*** a book last night. (action)

Krystal ***seems*** intelligent. (state)

A *verb* follows the *subject* of a sentence and can have an ***-ing, -ed,*** or ***-s*** word ending added to it, for example:

Kelvyn *(subj.) play**ed** (v.)* soccer *(n.).*

A verb changes form to inform the reader or listener as to when something occurred (verb tenses of time), such as:

write (s)	*wrote*	*written*	*writing*
play (s)	*played*	*playing*	

Main (Principal) Verbs

A *main verb,* also known as a *principal verb,* is the simplest 'stripped down' *verb form* (base or root word). A *verb* express *a continual* or *habitual action, general truth / fact*, or a *state of being* in a sentence. The *main verb* functions as the *present tense form* for all persons and numbers, but not the *third-person singular*, which uses the ***-s form***. Examples are:

*she **writes*** *he **plays***

Note: A *main verb* is the first *word form* listed in most English language dictionaries. The *main verb* can have *morphemes* called *affixes* attached to them either at the beginning of the *verb*, called *prefixes* (***re-, in-, un-, co-, miss-, un-***), or the ending, called *suffixes* (***-ing, -ion, -ation, -able, -ment***). The addition of such *morphemes* may change the word's form. Examples are:

believe (v.), *believ**ing*** (n., adj.), ***un**believ**able*** (adj.)

Active and Passive Voice

Voice refers to whether the *subject* of a sentence is performing the action, or is having the action done to it.

Active voice, also referred to as *normal voice,* refers to the <u>*subject*</u> performing the action, such as:

<u>Sir Edmond Hillary</u> ***climbed*** Mount Everest.

The *passive voice* places the entity that receives the action in the *subject* position of the sentence. This shifts the focus from the entity performing the action to the entity receiving the action. The construction of a *passive voice* sentence and examples are:

subject **+ auxiliary verb (be) +** <u>main verb</u> *(past participle*)*

The classroom **was** <u>*cleaned*</u>* by John.*

The main verb is **always** *in its past participle form.*

The Conjugation for Passive Voice

The *passive voice* can be formed in any *tense* or *future time* by following these simple examples (also see Table 20.):

Present Simple: ~ *am / are / is* + *past participle*

Present Continuous: ~ *is being / are being* + *past participle*

Present Perfect: ~ *has been / have been* + *past participle*

Present Perfect Continuous: ~ **has / have been being +** *past participle*

Past Simple: ~ *was / were* + *past participle*

Past Continuous: ~ *was being / were being* + *past participle*

Past Perfect: ~ *had been* + *past participle*

Past Perfect continuous: ~ *had been being* + *past participle*

Future Simple: ~ *will be* + *past participle*

Future Continuous: ~ *will be being* + *past participle*

Future Perfect: ~ *will have been* + *past participle*

Future Perfect Continuous: ~ **will have been being +** *past participle*

Note: *Modal verbs* can be used in the *passive voice*, such as: …**can be** <u>*loved*</u>… or …**might / could have been** <u>*avoided*</u>…

Table 20. Conjugation (link) for Passive Voice

Tense or future time		Examples	
Present	simple	active:	I call the cat Bonnie.
		passive:	*The cat* **is** <u>called</u> Bonnie.
	continuous	active:	The staff are dressing mannequins.
		passive:	*Mannequins* **are being** <u>dressed</u>.
	perfect	active:	We have invited our mates as well.
		passive:	*Our mates* **have been** <u>invited</u> as well.
	perfect continuous	active:	Fred has been cleaning his car.
		passive:	*His car* **has been being** <u>cleaned</u>.

Tense or future time		Examples	
Past	simple	active:	I named the horse Trigger.
		passive:	*The horse **was** <u>named</u> Trigger.*
	continuous	active:	Someone was making the coffee.
		passive:	*The coffee **was being** <u>made</u>.*
	perfect	active:	Peter had completed filming his documentary on Maori culture.
		passive:	*Filming his documentary on Maori culture **had been** <u>completed</u>.*
	perfect continuous	active:	Craig had been fueling the jet.
		passive:	*The jet **had been being** <u>fueled</u>.*
Future	simple	active:	The woman will wink at the child.
		passive:	*The child **will be** <u>winked</u> at.*
	continuous	active:	Jane will be driving the car.
		passive:	*The car **will be being** <u>driven</u>.*
	perfect	active:	Gary will have packed his lunch.
		passive:	*His lunch **will have been** <u>packed</u>.*
	perfect continuous	active:	I will have been soaking my new dentures.
		passive:	*My new dentures **will have been being** <u>soaked</u>.*

� Auxiliary Verbs ✄

An *auxiliary verb*, also known as a *helping verb*, determines the *mood*, *voice*, or *tense*, modifying the meaning of the *main verb* that they accompany in a *verb phrase*.

Primary Auxiliary Verbs:

'**be**' forms: *am, are, is, was, were, been, being*

'**do**' forms: *do, does, did*

'**have**' forms: have, *has, had, having*

Modal Auxiliary Verbs:

can	*could*	*may*	*might*	*will*
would	*shall*	*should*	*must*	*ought (to)*

Primary Auxiliary Verbs (be, do, have)

A *primary auxiliary verb* can be used as follows:

be*:   **be** + present participle (verb + -ing) = *progressive form*
        be + past participle = passive (voice)

do*:   **do, does**, or **did** + the basic (base) *verb form* can be
        used in *negative, emphasis*, or *interrogative* sentences.

have*: **have, has**, or **had** + past participle = *perfect form*

        *can also be used as a *main verb*.

Table 21. Primary Auxiliary Verbs

Primary Auxiliary (Helping) Verb Forms				
Base Form	Present Form	Past Form	Past Participle	Present Participle
be	am, are, is	was, were	been	being
do	do, does	did	—	—
have	have, has	had	—	having

Note: *Contracted verb forms* can be stacked. Examples are:

~ woud have:

   I'd've told her to study if I had been there.

~ will have:

   He'll've arrived by the time the presentation starts.

Primary Auxiliary Verb *'be'* and Its Forms

The *primary auxiliary verb 'be'* and its forms are used to create the *continuous / progressive form* of a *verb phrase*, indicating either a *short-term action* or an *action* that is still in progress, or to create a *passive voice*. Examples are:

He **is** <u>watching</u> football on TV. (continuous / progressive form)

Zebras **are** <u>eaten</u> by lions. (passive voice)

Here is the *main verb 'be'* and the different forms of the *'be' auxiliary verb* with examples:

The basic or base form (main verb):

be   In use:

>   To **be** or *not to* **be** kind is the question.

The present continuous forms and passive voice [**be** auxiliary *verb*]:

am: Used with the word *'I'* as the *subject:*

>   I **am** <u>playing</u> football now. (affirmative)
>   I **am** <u>called</u> lucky by my friends. (passive voice)
>   **Am** I <u>doing</u> this how you wanted? (interrogative)

   Use **I'm** as the contracted form of **I am***:*

>   **I'm** <u>eating</u> lunch now.

   Use **am not** for *negative sentences:*

>   I **am not** <u>dancing</u> tonight… never …~~amn't~~ dancing...

are: Used with the words **we**, **you**, **they** or a *plural noun phrase* as the *subject:*

>   They **are** <u>smiling</u> at me. (affirmative)
>   They **are** <u>shown</u> regularly. (passive voice)
>   **Are** you <u>coming</u> to my party this weekend?
>   (interrogative)
>   My twins **are** <u>wearing</u> the same clothes.
>   (plural noun phrase)

   Use **~'re** as the contracted form of **we are**, **you are** or **they are***:*

>   We**'re** <u>painting</u> the house next week.
>   You**'re** <u>going</u> to the park on Saturday.
>   They**'re** <u>cooking</u> New Zealand spring lamb.

   Use **are not**, or the contracted form **aren't**, for *negative sentences:*

>   We **are not** (aren't) <u>joking</u> around.
>   You **are not** (aren't) <u>flying</u> due to heavy rain.
>   They **are not** (aren't) <u>laughing</u> at my joke.

is: Used with the words *he, she*, *it* or a *singular noun phrase* as the *subject:*

> He *is* <u>reading</u> a book. (affirmative)
> He *is* <u>loaded</u> with homework. (passive voice)
> What *is* she <u>doing?</u> (interrogative)
> My patient *is* <u>wearing</u> a hospital gown.
> (singular noun phrase)

Use **~'s** as the contracted form of *he is, she is or it is:*

> He*'s* <u>practicing</u> the piano.
> She*'s* <u>studying</u> English now.
> It*'s* <u>raining</u> now.

Use *is not*, or the contracted form *isn't*, for *negative sentences:*

> He *is not* (*isn't*) <u>being</u> very nice at all.
> She *is not* (*isn't*) <u>wearing</u> her hat.
> It *is not* (*isn't*) <u>growing</u> well.

The past continuous forms and passive voice [*be auxiliary verb*]:

was: Used with the words *I, he, she*, *it* or a *singular noun phrase* as the *subject:*

> I *was* <u>making</u> cookies with my grandma. (affirmative)
> I *was* <u>worked</u> to the bone. (passive voice)
> *Was* it <u>snowing</u> all night? (interrogative)
> My wife *was* <u>snoring</u> all night. (singular noun phrase)

Note: There is no contracted form for *was*.

Use *was not*, or the contracted form *wasn't*, for *negative sentences:*

> I *was not* (*wasn't*) <u>having</u> fun at the opera.
> He *was not* (*wasn't*) <u>running</u> the race in top form.
> It *was not* (*wasn't*) <u>smoking</u> last time I checked.

were: Used with the words *we, you*, *they* or a *plural noun phrase* as the *subject:*

> We *were* <u>cheering</u> for our favorite team. (affirmative)
> You *were* <u>choked</u> by the smoke. (passive)
> *Were* you <u>drinking</u> all night? (interrogative)
> My parents *were* <u>bathing</u> at the spa last week.
> (plural noun phrase)

Note: There is no contracted form for **were**.

Use **were not**, or the contracted form **weren't**, for *negative sentences:*

> We **were not** (weren't) <u>serving</u> pasta.
>
> You **were not** (weren't) <u>singing</u> very well.
>
> They **were not** (weren't) <u>looking</u> at me.

Primary Auxiliary Verb *'do'* and Its Forms

The *primary auxiliary verb 'do'* and its forms are used to create *negatives*, *interrogatives*, and to show *emphasis*. Examples are:

> I **do not** <u>like</u> cabbage. (negative)
>
> **Do** you <u>work</u> for Google? (interrogative)
>
> I **did** <u>say</u> to you wait for me! (emphasis)

Here is the *main verb 'do'* and the different forms of the *'do' auxiliary verb* with examples:

The basic or base form (main verb):

> **do**   In use:
>
> > When I get home from school I **do** my homework.

The present simple forms [**do** *auxiliary verb*]:

> **do:**   Used with the **words** *I*, **you**, *we*, **they** or a *plural noun phrase* as the *subject*.
>
> An affirmative sentence doesn't normally use the *auxiliary verb 'do'* unless the word *'do'* is used for *emphasis:*
>
> > I like ice-cream. Or, I **do** <u>like</u> ice-cream. (emphasis)
> >
> > My friends **do** <u>enjoy</u> clubbing. (plural noun phrase)
>
> Use **do** in an interrogative (question):
>
> > **Do** you <u>avoid</u> eating spicy food?

Note: There is no contracted form for **do**.

Use **do not**, or the contracted form **don't**, for *negative sentences:*

> I **do not** (don't) <u>consider</u> chocolate as junk food.

does: Used with the words *he, she, it* or a *singular noun phrase* as the *subject*.

An affirmative sentence doesn't normally use the *auxiliary verb 'does'* unless the word *'does'* is used for *emphasis*:

> She sleeps often. Or, *she **does** sleep* often.
> (emphasis).

> *His dog **does** dig* in my garden...bugger!
> (singular noun phrase)

Use ***does*** in an interrogative (question):

> ***Does*** he visit his parents on the weekend?

Note: There is no contracted form for ***does***.

Use ***does not***, or the contracted form ***doesn't***, for *negative sentences*:

> He ***does not*** (doesn't) swim in the ocean.

The past simple form [***do*** *auxiliary verb*]:

did: Used with the words *I, you, we, they, he, she, it* or a *noun phrase* as the *subject*.

An affirmative sentence doesn't normally use the *auxiliary verb 'did'* unless the word *'did'* is used for *emphasis*:

> He drove me crazy. Or, *He **did** drive* me crazy.
> (emphasis)

> *My students **did** participate* well. (noun phrase)

Use ***did*** in an interrogative (question):

> ***Did*** they call me?

Note: There is no contracted form for ***did***.

Use ***did not***, or the contracted form ***didn't***, for *negative sentences*:

> I ***did not*** (didn't) shoot the ball at the buzzer.

Primary Auxiliary Verb *'have'* and Its Forms

The *primary auxiliary verb '**have**'* and its forms are used to create *affirmatives*, *negatives*, and *interrogatives* using the *perfect form* of *main verbs*. Examples are:

> I ***have not*** cleaned my room yet. (negative)

> ***Have*** you answered the questionnaire? (interrogative)

Here is the *main verb* **'have'** and the different forms of the **'have'** *auxiliary verb* with examples:

The basic or base form (main verb):

have In use:

To **have** or not to **have** happiness is but a choice.

The present perfect forms [**have** auxiliary verb]:

have: Used with the words *I, you, we, they* or a *plural noun phrase* as the *subject:*

I **have** *enjoyed* painting all my life. (affirmative)

Their children **have** *been* *talking* all night.
(plural noun phrase)

Use **have** in an interrogative (question):

Have *you* *seen* the new action movie?

Use **~'ve** as the contracted form of *I have*, **we have, you have** or **they have**:

*I'***ve** *filmed* many animal behaviors.

*You'***ve** *encouraged* me often.

*They'***ve** *drained* the pool to clean it.

Use **have not**, or the contracted form **haven't**, for *negative sentences:*

I **have not** *(haven't)* *extended* an invitation to him yet.

We **have not** *(haven't)* *gathered* here to be passive.

You **have not** *(haven't)* *healed* well.

has: Used with the words *he, she, it* or a *singular noun phrase* as the *subject:*

He **has** *instructed* me well. (affirmative)

My flight **has** *been* delayed. (singular noun phrase)

Use *has* in an interrogative (question):

Has *he* *traveled* extensively?

Use **~'s** as the contracted form of **he has, she has** or **It has**:

*He'***s** *played* on this team for months.

*She'***s** *won* the beauty-pageant three years running.

*It'***s** *worked* out well for everyone.

Use **has not**, or the contracted form **hasn't**, for *negative sentences:*

> He **has not** (*hasn't*) <u>listened</u> to me at all.
>
> She **has not** (*hasn't*) <u>changed</u> her opinion.
>
> It **has not** (*hasn't*) <u>nested</u> in that tree this year.

The past perfect form [**have** *auxiliary verb*]:

had Used with the words *I, you, we, they, he, she, it* or a *noun phrase* as the *subject:*

> They **had** <u>climbed</u> down from the tree. (affirmative)
>
> My girlfriend **had** <u>been</u> late. (noun phrase)

Use **had** in an interrogative (question):

> **Had** she <u>memorized</u> her notes?

Use **-'d** as the contracted form of *I had, you had, we had, they had, he had, she had* or *it had:*

> I**'d** <u>parked</u> there before.
>
> They**'d** <u>performed</u> to the best of their ability.
>
> He**'d** <u>queued</u> for hours in the rain.

Use **had not**, or the contracted form **hadn't**, for *negative sentences:*

> I **had not** (*hadn't*) <u>remembered</u> a thing.
>
> He **had not** (*hadn't*) <u>recognized</u> her.
>
> You **had not** (*hadn't*) <u>telephoned</u> beforehand!

Modal Auxiliary Verbs

A *modal auxiliary verb* is used to modify the meaning of the *main verb* allowing the expression of *necessity, obligation,* or *possibility.* A *modal auxiliary verb* can also form a *question* and a *negative.* The *modal auxiliary verbs* are:

can, could, and might

may and must

shall, should, and ought (to)

will

would

Each of the 10 *modal auxiliary verbs* have different strengths in their meaning with other similar modals, reflecting *stronger* or *weaker effect.*

Table 22. Modal Auxiliary Verbs

Examples of Modal Auxiliary Verbs (also see next section)					
can	cannot	can't	could	could not	couldn't
may	may not	mayn't	might	might not	mightn't
must	must not	mustn't	ought (to)	ought not	oughtn't
shall	shall not	shan't	should	should not	shouldn't
will	will not	won't	would	would not	wouldn't

Can, Could and *Might* - Used in an *affirmative* and *negative statement,* or *interrogative* (can and could mainly) with the words *I, you, we, they, he, she,* and *it,* or a *singular* or *plural noun phrase* as the *subject.*

Table 23. Modal Auxiliary Verbs 'Can', 'Could' and 'Might'

Modal	Negative	Meanings	Examples
can	cannot can't	ability	*I* **can** *speak* English well.
		permission	**Can** *we play* lacrosse today?
		possibility	*You* **can** *ask* for a raise if you like.
		request or offer	**Can** *you help* me, please? **Can** *I help* you?
could	could not couldn't	past ability	He **could** *play* football years ago, but his age has caught up to him.
		permission	I was wondering, **could** *I borrow* your car?
		future possibility	*It* **could** *rain* this afternoon. I suppose *I* **could** *take* my umbrella.
		request	I understand you may be busy, but **could** *you go* and buy some milk?
		suggestion	Q: What can I do to improve? A: *You* **could** *study* more!
might	might not mightn't	probability	*I* **might** *win* the lottery.
		possibility in the past	If you had studied more, *you* **might** *have passed* the exam!

May and *Must* - Used in an *affirmative* and *negative statement,* or *interrogative* with the words *I, you, we, they, he, she,* and *it,* or a *singular* or *plural noun phrase* as the *subject.*

Table 24. Modal Auxiliary Verbs 'May' and 'Must'

Modal	Negative	Meanings	Examples
may	may not	formal request, or permission	Q: *May* I *come* in, please? A: Yes, please come in. *May* I *be excused?*
		possibility in the future	I feel that I *may do* really well on the English exam. I feel pretty confident.
must	must not mustn't	obligation	He *must train* for the race if he has any chance to place well. I *mustn't drink* alcohol the night before a game. I'll let the team down.
		deduction	Q: Where is your homework? A: I *must have left* it at home.

Shall, Should and *Ought* (to) - Used in an *affirmative* and *negative statement,* or *interrogative* (shall and should mainly) with the words *I, you, we, they, he, she,* and *it,* or a *singular* or *plural noun phrase* as the *subject.*

Table 25. Modal Auxiliary Verbs 'Shall', 'Should' and 'Ought (to)'

Modal	Negative	Meanings	Examples
shall	shall not shan't	asking advice	What *shall* I *do* to make my classmates like me?
		suggestion	*Shall we eat* dinner before it's cold? *Shall* I *open* the door for you?
		future statement	All students *shall maintain* a 100% attendance record to pass my class.
should	should not	offering advice	You *should practice* often to become talented at football. *Should you need* assistance, ask!
	shouldn't	expectation	My acceptance letter to university *should arrive* today.
ought (to)	ought not (to)	suggestion	You *ought to speak* at the reunion.

Will - Used in an *affirmative* and *negative statement*, or *interrogative* with the words *I, you, we, they, he, she,* and *it*, or a *singular* or *plural noun phrase* as the *subject*.

Table 26. Modal Auxiliary Verb 'Will'

Modal	Negative	Meanings	Examples
will	will not won't	to insist	*I will not* change his mind.
		intention or promise	*He will take* an English exam today. *She will call* you as soon as she arrives!
		certainty in the future	*I will be* 50 next month.
		prediction	I doubt if *I'll climb* Mount Cook ever again.

Would - Used in an *affirmative* and *negative statement*, or *interrogative* with the words *I, you, we, they, he, she,* and *it*, or a *singular* or *plural noun phrase* as the *subject*. [the word *'would'* is often contracted to *'d*]

Table 27. Modal Auxiliary Verb 'Would'

Modal	Negative	Meanings	Examples
would or ~'d	would not wouldn't	habit performed in the past	When we were children, *we would* always *have* an annual family reunion where we would play touch-football in the backyard.
		cautionary insistence	*I would suggest* you wear your life-jacket if you go out on the water!
		polite question	*Would you like* another plate of spaghetti and meatballs?
		preference	*I would* rather *be* inconspicuous.

QUOTE:

"The English language is nobody's special property. It is the property of the imagination: it is the property of the language itself."

Derek Walcott

✤ Regular and Irregular Verbs ✤

A *regular verb*, also known as a *weak verb*, is used to describe an *action*, *state* or *occurrence*. The form of a *main verb* can change by adding *-d* or *-ed*, or by changing *-y* to *-i* (if the *verb* ends in a consonant + *-y*) and then adding *-ed*, to create a *past simple tense* and *past participle* (A *verb* that functions as an *adjective*). Examples are:

    Adding *-d :* I *save* money. ⟹ I *saved* money.

    Adding *-ed :* I *walk* to school. ⟹ I *walked* to school.

    Present Simple: I *study* English.

    Past Simple: I *studied* English. *(I study* ⟹ *I stud̶y̶ + i + ed)*

    Past Participle: I have *studied* English.

An *irregular verb*, also known as a *strong verb*, is used when the *past simple tense* and *past participle* cannot end with *-d* or *-ed*. Examples are:

    Present Simple: I *eat* breakfast. *(I eat + ̶e̶d̶)*

    Past Simple: I *ate* breakfast.

    Past Participle: I have *eaten* breakfast.

There are about 200 common *irregular verbs* in the English language. Many others have become obsolescent or obsolete. Below is a sample list of the more common *irregular verbs* in use:

Table 28. Irregular Verbs (a more complete list is in the Appendix)

Base Form	Past Simple	Past Participle		Base Form	Past Simple	Past Participle
begin	began	begun		have	had	had
do	did	done		learn*	learnt learned	learnt learned
draw	drew	drawn		leave	left	left
dream*	dreamt dreamed	dreamt dreamed		ring	rang	rung
drive	drove	driven		rise	rose	risen
eat	ate	eaten		see	saw	seen
freeze	froze	frozen		sing	sang	sung
go	went	gone		swear	swore	sworn

*Some *verbs* can be both *regular* or *irregular*.

Verb Tense and Future Time

The *tense* expressed by a *verb* indicates *the time of the action* or *its state of being*. Technically, the English language has *two verb tenses* and a method to reference *future time:*

Present Tense: A *verb tense* that expresses a *continual* or *habitual action, general truth / fact,* or *state of being*, with at least part of the element occurring in the *present time*.

Past Tense: A *verb tense* that expresses a *continual* or *habitual action* or *state of being*, that occurred at a *definite time in the past*, which does NOT extend into the *present time*.

Future Time*: A form that expresses a *continual* or *habitual action* or *state of being* that has not yet begun.

*The English language uses *modal auxiliaries*, *present and past tense forms*, and *adverbials of time*, to express an action that has not yet begun. Although there is no *future tense* in the English language, the correct *verb form 'future time'* is commonly referred to as a *future tense*.

Table 29. Verb Tense and Future Time Using the Verb 'Write'

	Simple	Continuous (Progressive)	Perfect	Perfect Continuous (Perfect Progressive)
Present	I write	I am writing	I have written	I have been writing
Past	I wrote	I was writing	I had written	I had been writing
Future	I will write	I will be writing	I will have written	I will have been writing

> ***QUOTE:***
>
> *"Arguments over grammar and style are often as fierce as those over Windows versus Mac OS, and as fruitless as Coca-Cola versus Pepsi and boxer underwear versus briefs."*
>
> *Jack Lynch*

Present Simple

Use the *present simple tense* to express *a situation, general truth / fact, a state of being* or *event* that exists right now, at the time of speaking.

A situation, truth, fact, state or event

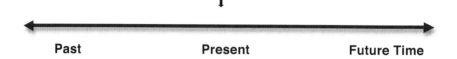

| Past | Present | Future Time |

Table 30. **Structure for Present Simple Tense**

subject pronoun, or noun phrase (or clause)	Affirmative *subject +* *main verb*	Negative *subject + aux. +* *not + main verb*		Interrogative *aux. + subject +* *main verb*		
	main verb	*aux. +* *not*	*main* *verb*	*aux.*	*subject*	*main* *verb*
I, you, we, they	admire crave enjoy live deliver etc.	do not don't	admire crave enjoy live deliver etc.	do	I, you, we, they	admire crave enjoy live deliver etc.
he, she, it	*main verb +* **s** *~ There are* *exceptions.* orbit**s**, eat**s**, etc.	does not doesn't		does	he, she, it	

Affirmatives:

> I <u>admire</u> volunteers.
> The Earth <u>orbits</u> around the Sun.

Negatives:

> She **does not** (*doesn't*) <u>crave</u> chocolate.
> They **do not** (*don't*) <u>enjoy</u> boating.

Interrogatives:

> **Does** Ralf <u>live</u> here?
> **Do** you <u>deliver</u> pizza?

Use the *present simple tense* to express *a single continual* or *habitual action*. At least part of the element must occur in the *present time*. *Frequency adverbs* are often used, such as: *often, daily, usually,* etc.

A single continual or habitual action

Affirmatives:

> I *entertain* guests often.
>
> He *paints* seascapes every day.
>
> We *shear* sheep every week.

Negatives:

> I **do not** (*don't*) *smoke* cigars often.
>
> She **does not** (*doesn't*) *practice* judo daily.
>
> They **do not** (*don't*) *go shopping* every week.

Interrogatives:

> **Do** you *recycle* newspapers weekly?
>
> **Does** she usually *knit* socks for all her grandchildren's gifts?

Table 31. Using 'be' Verbs as Main Verbs

	Subject	Main verb*	Neg.	Complement
Affirmative	I	am	—	twenty-one
	you, we, they	are	—	late
	he, she, it	is	—	smart
Negative	I	am	not	nervous
	you, we, they	are	not	early
	he, she, it	is	not	fat
Interrogative	am	I	—	right
	are	you, we, they	—	ready
	is	he, she, it	—	shrewd

*The **'be'** verb changes when it is used with another tense. For example: **'is'** and **'am'** → **'was'** or **'are'** → **'were'** for the *past tense*.

Past Simple

Use the *past simple tense* to express *a single event, action*, or *a series of completed events or actions* (1st, 2nd, 3rd, etc.) that began and ended at a particular time in the past.

The *past simple tense* can also be used to express *an extended duration of time that occurred in the past*, usually conveyed with words or phrases: *for* (~ 5-years, ~ fifty-years), *all* (~ day, ~ week, ~ year), etc.

single event or action

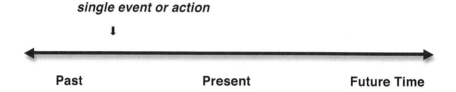

| **Past** | **Present** | **Future Time** |

Table 32. Structure for Past Simple Tense

subject pronoun, or noun phrase (or clause)	Affirmative **subject + main verb + ed**	Negative **subject + aux. + not + main verb**		Interrogative **aux. + subject + main verb**		
	main verb + ed	*aux. + not*	*main verb*	*aux.*	*subject*	*main verb*
I, you, we, they, he, she, it	played studied ate* ran* etc.	did not didn't	play study eat* run* etc.	did	I, you, we, they, he, she, it	play study eat* run* etc.
	irregular verbs					

Affirmatives:

> I *played* football at noon, *took* a shower, then *went* home.

> They *ate* fish and chips last night.

Negative:

> My sister **did not** (didn't) *study* Spanish last Tuesday.

Interrogative:

> **Did** you *run* last week?

Future Simple

Use the *future simple* (*time*) to describe a *single event* or *action* that is planned and yet to occur.

single event or action

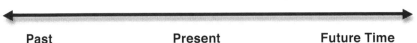

Past	Present	Future Time

Table 33. Structure for Future Simple Time

subject pronoun, or noun phrase (or clause)	Affirmative subject + aux. + main verb		Negative subject + aux. + not + main verb		Interrogative aux. + subject + main verb		
		aux.	aux. + not	main verb	aux.	subject	main verb
I, you, we, they, he, she, it	will (~'ll)		will not won't	call	will	I, you, we, they, he, she, it	call
I, we	shall		shan't	help	shall	I, we	help
I	am (~'m) going to		am not going to	coach	am	I (~ going to)	coach
you, we, they	are (~'re) going to		are not (aren't) going to	eat play	are	you, we, they (~ going to)	eat play
he, she, it	is (~'s) going to		is not (isn't) going to	etc.	is	he, she, it (~ going to)	etc.

Affirmative:

> *I **will** (shall) call* Henry next Tuesday.

Negative:

> *He **will not** (won't) coach* soccer later.

Interrogative:

> ***Will** you (shall we) play* football next Saturday?

Present Continuous

Use the *present continuous tense*, also known as the *present progressive tense*, to describe a *single event* or *action* that began in the recent past, has been continuous to the moment of speaking or writing, and is likely to end some time in the future.

The *present continuous tense* can also be used to *describe* or *express* a *general activity* that is ongoing, or planned, but not necessarily being done at this moment in time.

single event or action

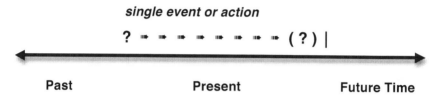

| Past | Present | Future Time |

Table 34. Structure for Present Continuous Tense

subject pronoun, or noun phrase (or clause)	Affirmative **subject + aux. + present participle**		Negative **subject + aux. + not + present participle**		Interrogative **aux. + subject + present participle**		
	aux.		*aux. + not*	*present participle*	*aux.*	*subject*	*present participle*
I	am (~'m)		am not	mov-ing	am	I	mov-ing
you, we, they	are (~'re)		are not aren't	hurt-ing los-ing	are	you, we, they	hurt-ing los-ing
he, she, it	is (~'s)		is not isn't	etc.	is	he, she, it	etc.

Affirmative:

　　The Roberts **are** <u>moving</u> furniture now.

Negative:

　　She **is not** (isn't) <u>hurting</u> anyone on purpose.

Interrogative:

　　Are they <u>losing</u> weight for the upcoming boxing matches?

Ongoing:

　　We **are** <u>learning</u> to ski this week. (time unknown)

Past Continuous

Use the *past continuous tense*, also known as the *past progressive tense*, to describe an *event* or *action* that was already in progress when it was interrupted by another *event* or *action*.

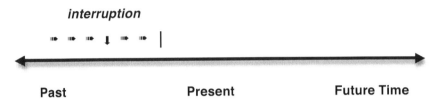

interruption

Past   Present   Future Time

Table 35. Structure for Past Continuous Tense

subject pronoun, or noun phrase (or clause)	Affirmative *subject +* *aux. + present* *participle*		Negative *subject +* *aux. + not +* *present participle*		Interrogative *aux. +* *subject +* *present participle*		
	aux.		*aux. + not*	*present participle*	*aux.*	*subject*	*present participle*
I, he, she, it	was		was not wasn't	add-ing play-ing	was	I, he, she, it	add-ing play-ing
you, we	were		were not weren't	stack-ing etc.	were	you, we, they	stack-ing etc.

Affirmatives:

> She **was** <u>knitting</u> sweaters for her two children.

> The apprentice cooks **were** <u>adding</u> milk and eggs to the cake recipe when the Sous-chef walked in.

Negatives:

> I **was not** (*wasn't*) <u>playing</u> football when the whistle blew.

> You **were not** (*weren't*) <u>making</u> tea when your dad arrived.

Interrogatives:

> **Was** he <u>barbequing</u> sausages when his brother showed up?

> **Were** they <u>stacking</u> bricks when the supervisor called?

The *past continuous tense* can also be used in two or more parts of a sentence to show that the *event* or *action* was in progress simultaneously, but do not influence each other.

two simultaneous events or actions

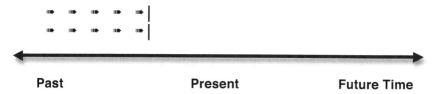

Past   **Present**   **Future Time**

Examples:

> John **was** <u>studying</u> British-American history while *Jim* **was** <u>reading</u> the newspaper.
>
> *You* **were** <u>eating</u> lunch while *they* **were** <u>shopping</u>.

The Humor of the English Language

1. I did not object to the object being lain at my feet.

2. The insurance claim was assessed as invalid for the invalid.

3. If teachers taught, why didn't preachers praught?

4. There was a row between the sea-scouts and the organizers on which row they should row in.

5. If you are close to the door then you should close it!

6. Does a buck's adrenaline increase when the does are close by?

7. A tailor and his sewer fell down a deep sewer.

8. Is it possible that a well-trained sow can sow seeds on the farm?

9. The dentist injected a number of shots into the patient's jaw, making his jaw number.

Future Continuous

Use the *future continuous* (*time*), also known as the *future progressive time*, to describe an *ongoing event* or *action* that will be happening at a particular time in the future. The *future continuous* (*time*) will contain either the verb phrase *'will be'* or *'shall be'* or *'going to be'* as well as a *present participle*.

ongoing event or action at a particular time

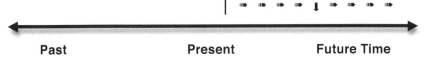

| Past | Present | Future Time |

Table 36. Structure for Future Continuous Time

subject pronoun, or noun phrase (or clause)	Affirmative *subject +* *aux. +* *aux. +* *present* *participle*	Negative *subject +* *aux. + not +* *aux. + present* *participle*		Interrogative *aux. +* *subject +* *aux. +* *present participle*			
	aux. + aux.	*aux. +* *not +* *aux.*	*present* *participle*	*aux.*	*subject*	*aux.*	*present* *participle*
I, you, we, they, he, she, it	will (~'ll) shall be	will / shall not be won't / shan't be	writ-ing clear-ing do-ing etc.	will shall	I, you, we, they, he, she, it	be	writ-ing clear-ing do-ing etc.

Affirmative:

> *I **will be** writing* in my journal this afternoon.

Negatives:

> *I **will not be** (won't be) clearing* the leaves from my garden when you return from work.

> *The girls **are not** (aren't) **going to be** doing* dishes when their friends arrive.

Interrogative:

> What ***shall** you **be** doing* when I return from holiday?

The *future continuous tense* can also be used to express *two or more events* or *actions* in the same sentence that are occurring simultaneously.

two simultaneous events or actions

Past   Present   Future Time

Examples:

> *John* **will be** <u>studying</u> fashion design while *Jim* **will be** <u>studying</u> the art of Ikebana.

> *I am* **going to be** <u>visiting</u> my doctor while *Jude is* **going to be** <u>attending</u> a job interview.

QUOTE:

"I don't know the rules of grammar ... If you're trying to persuade people to do something, or buy something, it seems to me you should use their language, the language they use every day, the language in which they think. We try to write in the vernacular."

David Ogilvy

Present Perfect

Use the *present perfect tense* to describe a *completed event* or *action* where the exact time is unknown.

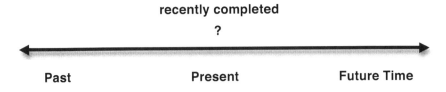

recently completed

?

Past   Present   Future Time

Table 37. Structure for Present Perfect Tense

subject pronoun, or noun phrase	Affirmative subject + aux. + past participle	Negative subject + aux. + not + past participle		Interrogative aux. + subject + past participle		
(or clause)	*aux.*	*aux. + not*	*past participle*	*aux.*	*subject*	*past participle*
I, you, we, they	have (~'ve)	have not haven't	seen (irregular) earn-ed	have	I, you, we, they	seen (irregular) earn-ed
he, she, it	has (~'s)	has not hasn't	eras-ed defus-ed etc.	has	he, she, it	eras-ed defus-ed etc.

Affirmative:

> We **have** just <u>seen</u> a child from Africa that we may adopt.

Negative:

> She **has not** (hasn't) <u>earned</u> our respect yet.

Interrogative:

> **Have** they <u>defused</u> the situation?

Use the *present perfect tense* to describe an *event* or *action* that began in the past where the exact time is unknown, and there is a connection to the present.

event or action still ongoing

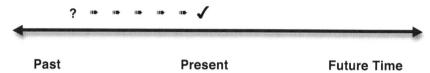

Past　　　　　　　　**Present**　　　　　　　　**Future Time**

Examples:

*I **have** delivered* newspapers since I was young.

*It **has** hailed* off-and-on all week.

*He **has** eaten* spicy food since he was introduced to it some time ago.

Why the English Language is Difficult to Understand.

Quicksand works slowly, boxing rings are square, and a guinea-pig is neither from Guinea nor is it a pig, writers write, but fingers don't fing, and hammers don't ham.

There is no egg in eggplant or ham in hamburger; neither is there an apple nor pine in pineapple.

If a vegetarian eats vegetables, does a humanitarian eat humans?

We ship by truck, and send cargo by ship.

We have noses that run and feet that smell.

One goose, two geese. One moose two meese?

The bandage was wound around the wound.

The farm was used to produce produce.

Since there is no time like the present, he thought it was time to present the present.

Past Perfect

Use the *past perfect tense* to express a *completed event* or *action* that occurred before another *action* in the past.

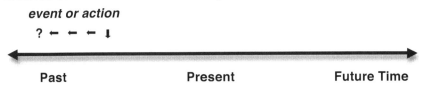

Subject pronoun, or noun phrase (or clause)	Affirmative subject + aux. + past participle	Negative subject + aux. + not + past participle		Interrogative aux. + subject + past participle		
	aux.	aux. + not	past participle	aux.	subject	past participle
I, you, we, they, he, she, it	had (~'d)	had not hadn't	learnt (irregular) edit-ed join-ed divert-ed etc.	had	I, you, we, they, he, she, it	learnt (irregular) edit-ed join-ed divert-ed etc.

Table 38. Structure for Past Perfect Tense

Affirmatives:

He **had** *learnt* the art of taxidermy from his grandfather before he opened his business.

She **had** *edited* the book many times prior to publishing.

Negatives:

They **had not** (hadn't) *joined* scouts.

We **had not** (hadn't) *sought* reconciliation.

Interrogatives:

Had they *diverted* funds before the scandal?

Had he *bought* a car before he owned his Harley Davidson?

Future Perfect

Use the *future perfect* (*time*) to describe an *event* or *action* in the past from a viewpoint or position in the future.

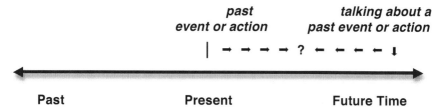

	past **event or action**	**talking about a** **past event or action**
	| → → → → ? ← ← ← ← ↓	
	←――――――――――――――――→	
Past	**Present**	**Future Time**

Table 39. Structure for Future Perfect Time

subject pronoun, or noun phrase (or clause)	Affirmative **subject +** **aux. + aux.** **+ past** **participle**	Negative **subject +** **aux. + not +** **aux. +** **past participle**		Interrogative **aux. +** **subject +** **aux. +** **past participle**			
	aux. + aux.	*aux. +* *not +* *aux.*	*past* *participle*	*aux.*	*subject*	*aux.*	*past* *participle*
I, you, we, they, he, she, it	will (~'ll) shall have ~'ll've	will / shall not have won't / shan't have ~'ll not 've	eaten (irregular) finish-ed reward-ed shipp-ed etc.	will	I, you, we, they, he, she, it	have	eaten (irregular) finish-ed reward-ed shipp-ed etc.

Affirmatives:

> *I **will have** <u>eaten</u>* dinner prior to going to the movies.

> This time next week *I **will have** <u>finished</u>* painting my house.

Negative:

> *They **will not** (won't) **have** <u>shipped</u>* the package by Monday.

Interrogative:

> ***Will** you **have** <u>secured</u>* a seat by the time I arrive at the concert?

Present Perfect Continuous

Use the *present perfect continuous tense*, also known as the *present perfect progressive tense*, to express an *event* or *action* that has began in the past and has recently completed, or has continued up to the present.

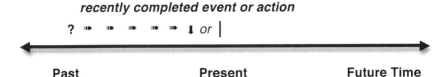

Table 40. Structure for Present Perfect Continuous Tense

subject pronoun, or noun phrase	Affirmative *subject + aux. + aux. + present participle*	Negative *subject + aux. + not + aux. + present participle*		Interrogative *aux. + subject + aux. + present participle*		
(or clause)	*aux. + aux.*	*aux. + not + aux.*	*present participle*	*aux.*	*subject*	*aux.*	*present participle*
I, you, we, they	have (~'ve) been	have not been haven't been	do-ing clean-ing tak-ing	have	I, you, we, they	been	do-ing clean-ing tak-ing
he, she, it	has (~'s) been	has not been hasn't been	rest-ing etc.	has	he, she, it		rest-ing etc.

Affirmatives:

I **have been** <u>co-writing</u> a book. Now I can take a holiday.

What **have** you **been** <u>doing</u>? I **have been** <u>cleaning</u> my car.

Negative:

She seems depressed. I believe she **has not been** (*hasn't been*) <u>taking</u> her medication.

Interrogative:

They look exhausted. **Have** they **been** <u>resting</u> well?

Use the *present perfect continuous tense* to express the *idea* that a situation is still in progress up until now.

**situation in   until
progress   now**

? ⫸ ⫸ ⫸ ⫸ ⫸

←――――――――――――――――――――――――――――――→

Past   **Present**   **Future Time**

Affirmatives:

I **have been** <u>reading</u> A Tale of Two Cities by Charles Dickens for several months.

He **has been** <u>feeling</u> really tired since working a double shift.

Negatives:

We **have not been** (haven't been) <u>feeling</u> one-hundred percent recently.

He **has not been** (hasn't been) <u>studying</u> since Monday.

Interrogatives:

Have they **been** <u>waiting</u> here for days?

Has Janet **been** <u>designing</u> her new home over the last few months?

QUOTE:

"Would mankind [humankind] be but contented without the continual use of that little but significant pronoun 'mine' or 'my own', with what luxurious delight might they revel in the property of others! ... But if envy makes me sicken at the sight of everything that is excellent out of my own possession, then will the sweetest food be sharp as vinegar, and every beauty will in my depraved eyes appear as deformity."

Sarah Fielding

Past Perfect Continuous

Use the *past perfect continuous tense*, also known as the *past perfect progressive tense*, to express an *event* or *action* that occurred over an extended period of time that had been happening before something else happened.

ongoing event / events or action / actions

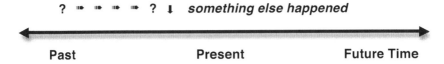

| Past | Present | Future Time |

Table 41. Structure for Past Perfect Continuous Tense

subject pronoun, or noun phrase (or clause)	Affirmative subject + aux. + aux. + present participle		Negative subject + aux. + not + aux. + present participle		Interrogative aux. + subject + aux. + present participle		
	aux. + aux.		*aux. + not + aux.*	*present participle*	*aux.*	*subject*	*aux.*	*present participle*
I, you, we, they, he, she, it	had (~'d) been		had not been \ hadn't been	rid-ing fill-ing plann-ing etc.	had	I, you, we, they, he, she, it	been	rid-ing fill-ing plann-ing etc.

Affirmative:

> It **had been** <u>snowing</u> for hours.

Negative:

> Kathy **had not been** (hadn't been) <u>working</u> very long when major changes in organizational structure were implemented.

Interrogative:

> For how long **had** he **been** <u>planning</u> the festival when a city bylaw was introduced disallowing such festivals?

Future Perfect Continuous

Use the *future perfect continuous* (*time*), also known as the *future perfect progressive* (*time*), to express an *event* or *action* that is in progress and will continue sometime into the future, often prior to another.

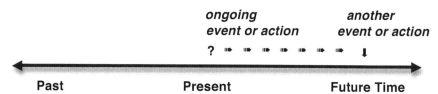

	ongoing event or action		another event or action

Past   Present   Future Time

Table 42. Structure for Future Perfect Continuous Time

subject pronoun, or noun phrase (or clause)	Affirmative **subject + aux. + aux. + aux. + present participle**	Negative **subject + aux. + not + aux. + aux. + present participle**		Interrogative **aux. + subject + aux. + aux. + present participle**			
	aux. + aux. + aux.	*aux. + not + aux. + aux.*	*present participle*	*aux.*	*subject*	*aux. + aux.*	*present participle*
I, you, we, they, he, she, it	will (~'ll) shall have been ~'ll've been	will not / shall not have been won't / shan't have been	train-ing resourc- ing runn-ing etc.	will shal l	I, you, we, they, he, she, it	have been	train-ing resourc- ing runn-ing etc.

Affirmative:

> He **will have been** <u>training</u> pilots for two-years by next month.

Negative:

> She **will not** (won't) **have been** <u>resourcing</u> companies with qualified staff for six months by the end of the year.

Interrogative:

> **Will** they **have been** <u>running</u> marathons by the time the first marathon starts this year?

63

�֍ Subject Verb Agreement �֍

To identify the correct agreement between a *subject* and a *verb*, the *subject* must be identified. This can be achieved in two steps. First, find the *verb* (the action) [or state of being]. Second, find the *subject* by identifying who or what is performing that action. In the example below, the word *'rode'* reflects the action performed, so *'rode'* is the *verb*. The entity who *'rode'* the bike is *James*, so *James* is the *subject*.

> *James* (sub.) *rode* (v.) his bike down the road.
>
> **Hint:** If a word precedes the word 'of ' then it is most likely the subject, such as:
>
> > *The herd* (sub.) <u>of</u> cows *ate* (v.) stored winter silage.
>
> In this example the word *'ate'* is the *verb* (the action). It may seem like the *'cows'* are the *subject*, but this is not the case. It is the *'herd'* that performed the action, so *'herd'* is the subject.

The *'be'* verbs (non-action verbs) are: *be, am, are, is, was, were, being* and *been*. The *'be'* verbs reflect a *'state of being'*, rather than an action that is being performed. To choose the correct *'be'* verb, the *subject* must be identified. Examples are:

> *He* (sub.) *is / was* (v.) here. *They* (sub.) *are / were* (v.) here.
> (not *He ~~are / were~~...*)   (not *They ~~is / was~~...*)
>
> *The bushel* (sub.) of apples *is / was* (v.) on the wagon.
> (*'The bushel'* is the *subject* not ~~apples [are]~~...)

Additional examples of specific *subject verb agreement* with the use of *indefinite pronouns* are:

Anyone, Everyone, Someone, ...

Indefinite pronouns such as *'anyone'*, *'anybody'*, *'someone'*, *'somebody'*, *'no one'* and *'nobody'* are *singular* [also sound *singular*] and therefore require an agreeable *singular verb*. The pronouns *everyone* and *everybody* are often seen to mean more than one person and sound plural, however, they are always treated as *singular*. Examples are:

> *Somebody has* <u>left</u> a handbag on the counter.
>
> *Everyone has* <u>completed</u> his or her assignment for this week.

Some *indefinite pronouns* such as *'some'* or *'all'*, can be either *singular* or *plural,* depending on whether they are referring to something that is either *countable* or *uncountable*. Examples are:

> *Some* of the beads *are* <u>missing</u>. (beads ➡ countable)
>
> *All* of the air *is* <u>polluted</u>. (air ➡ uncountable)

The indefinite pronoun *'none'* can be either *singular* or *plural*. If the *object* in the *prepositional phrase* is *singular*, then a *singular verb* is used. If the *object* in the *prepositional phrase* is *plural*, then a *plural verb* is used. Examples are:

None of the food **is** spicy. (food ➝ singular)

None of the employees **are** complaining. (employees ➝ plural)

None of the pilots **have** done their* annual training.

*The word their precludes the use of the *singular verb*.

The indefinite pronoun *'each'* [of] is *singular* and requires a *singular verb;* however, the word *'each'* is often followed by a *prepositional phrase* ending in a plural word, which often does cause confusion, such as:

Each of *the boys* **wears** a blue necktie with his uniform.

Together with, As well as, Along with

Phrases such as *'together with', 'as well as',* and *'along with'* do not have the same meaning as the word *'and'.* In the example below, the phrase *'as well as'* modifies the preceding word *'student',* but the phrase does not compound the *subjects,* as does the word *'and'.* Examples are:

The student, **as well as** his classmates, **is** going to a rugby game.

The student **and** his brothers **are** going to the basketball game.

Neither and Either

The indefinite pronouns *'neither'* (*negative*) and *'either'* (*positive*) almost always require *singular verbs*, even though they seem to be referring to two things. Examples are:

Do you want to eat or rest? **Neither** is what I really want to do.

Student: Teacher! Which textbook do you want me to open?

Teacher: **Either is** OK with me so long as you are studying.

Informally, the indefinite pronouns *'neither'* or *'either',* when paired with the preposition *'of',* [sometimes known as an of-pronoun], can optionally take either a *singular* or *plural verb* [this grammar rule is currently debatable]. However, the *pronoun* and *preposition* pairing must precede either a *plural pronoun* or a *plural noun phrase*. Examples are:

Neither of them **is (are)** studying.

Neither of the cows **has been (have been)** milked yet.

Either of the students **is (are)** welcome to attend.

Nor and Or

The conjunction *'or' does not conjoin*. When either *'nor'* or *'or'* is used, the *subject* closest to the *verb* determines the *singular* or *plural* state of the *verb*. Whether the *subject* comes before or after the *verb* doesn't matter; the proximity determines the usage. Examples are:

Either John <u>or</u> his **classmates** ← **are** <u>going</u> to sweep the floor.

Neither my classmates <u>nor</u> my **class-captain** ← **is** <u>going</u> to attend.

Are either ➡ my **classmates** <u>or</u> my teacher responsible?

Neither my teacher <u>nor</u> my **classmates** ← **are** available!

There and Here

The adverbs (of place) *'there'* and *'here'* are never *subjects*. They are often used to construct expletive sentences. Find the subject in the sentence and then apply the agreeable verb. In the following, the subject follows the verb, but still determines the verb's numerical state:

There **are** <u>three reasons</u> (det. + plural subject) why this won't work.

There **is** <u>no reason</u> (det. + singular subject) for any change.

Verbs in the Present Tense

A *verb* in the *present tense* for a *singular subject*, such as *'he'*, *'she'*, and *'it'* (third-person), or any alternative to these, requires an *'s'* ending.

A *verb* in the *present tense* for a *plural subject*, such as *they*, *we*, or any alternative to these, doesn't have an *'s'* ending. Examples are:

He loves to study English every day!

They love to walk on the beach on hot Sunday afternoons.

Nouns Ending with 's'

Some *nouns* that end with the letter *'s'* are *plural* and require a *plural verb*. Examples are:

My **assets were** liquidated when bad times hit.

The average students' **grades have** <u>gone</u> up dramatically since last term.

Our **hearts go** out to all those who lost their lives and possessions during the devastating tsunami.

Some *nouns* that end with the letter *'s'* appear to be plural, but are really *singular* and require *singular verbs*. Examples are:

The ongoing **news** about the Economy **is** not so good.

Herpes is a dangerous viral disease affecting the skin or nervous system.

Fractional Expressions

Fractional expressions, such as: *'half of'*, *'part of'*, *'percentage of'*, or *'majority of'*, can either be *singular* or *plural*, depending on their meaning [This is also true for the words: *all, any, some, more,* and *most,* when they act as a subject.]. Furthermore, sums and products of mathematical processes are expressed as *singular* and require *singular verbs.* Examples are:

Some of the students **are** still not happy with their performance.

A large percentage of the senior class **is** _taking_ their final exams today.

Two-fifths of the teachers **have** 20-years or more experience.

Half of the school **was** _destroyed_ by the Earthquake.

Forty percent of the students **are** in favor of the new uniforms.

Sixty percent of the student body **is** in favor of a new English language department wing.

It's not that easy! **One plus one is** not always two.

Five times four **divided by two is** (or *equals*) ten.

The expression *'more than one'* is also expressed as *singular,* such as:

More than one student **has** _tried_ to outsmart his teacher at one time or another; the emphasis is on 'tried'. You're not so unique!

Positive Verses Negative Subject

If a sentence compounds a *positive* and a *negative subject* and one is *plural,* the other *singular,* the *verb* should agree with the *positive subject.* Examples are:

The Judo team members, but not their coach, **have** _decided_ to attend a professional match next week.

It is not the staff members, but **the principal**, who **decides** on major issues.

It was **the politician**, not his party's ideas, that **has** _provoked_ the students to organize a sit-in.

PART FIVE — Adverbs (adv.)

Adverb Use

An *adverb* is a word that describes and clarifies a *verb*. An *adverb* can also *modify an adjective* or *another adverb*.

An *adverb modifies a verb*. Examples are:

John drove ***quickly***.

I ***almost*** fell asleep.

An *adverb* modifying an *adjective* usually precedes the *adjective*. Examples are:

John's English class was ***really*** great.

Japanese students are ***very*** clever!

An *adverb* modifying another *adverb* usually precedes the word it is modifying. Examples are:

John drove ***quite*** quickly up the street.

The answer you gave was ***really*** rather simple.

Adverb Types

There are five (5) main types of *adverbs*. These are: *degree, manner, place, frequency,* and *time.*

Adverbs of *degree*

These *adverbs* provide information on *how much* of something is done, such as:

almost, completely, deeply, entirely, fully, little, most, much, quite, rather, really, so, totally, too, very, etc.

Examples:

They were ***completely*** exhausted from three days of nonstop study.

We were ***totally*** prepared for the English exam.

Adverbs of *manner*

These *adverbs* provide information on *how* something happens or is done, such as:

carefully, enthusiastically, fast, gracefully, hard, how, impatiently, politely, quietly, slowly, so, stealthily, etc.

Examples:

I have (I've) noticed that my mom works **hard**.

John spoke **quietly** as he walked **slowly** past the sleeping bear.

Adverbs of *place*

These *adverbs* provide information on *where* something happened, happens, or may happen, such as:

about, above, behind, below, downstairs, far, here, indoors, near, outside, towards, there, where, etc.

Examples:

He ran **downstairs**, so he would be on-time.

I will meet you **outside** after the exam.

Adverbs of *frequency*

These *adverbs* provide information on *how often* that something happens, such as:

Definite: annually, daily, hourly, nightly, yearly, etc.

Indefinite: always, generally, normally, occasionally, regularly, seldom, sometimes, usually, etc.

Examples:

The school was moderated **annually**.

He **seldom** comes to school early.

Adverbs of *time*

These *adverbs* provide information on *when* something occurs, such as:

already, before, first, finally, late, now, previously, since, still, then, today, tomorrow, tonight, yesterday, yet, etc.

Examples:

Mary finished her English exam **first**.

I arrive **late** for most classes.

❊ Other Uses ❊

An *adverbs* can also be used to:

Add or to limit:

also, either, else, neither, only, too, ...

Reflect a viewpoint:

mentally, morally, officially, personally, strictly, ...

Link ideas:

firstly, however, nevertheless, so, therefore, ...

Reflect an opinion:

actually, fortunately, oddly, perhaps, strangely, surely, ...

❊ Adverb Intensifiers ❊

An *adverb* can function as *an intensifier* reflecting a greater or lesser emphasis to something. These *intensifying adverbs* have three different functions. These are:

Emphasizer:

Susan **really** doesn't believe she will pass her exam even though she studied all night.

The English exam will be difficult, **for sure**!

Amplifier:

The exam supervisor **completely** rejected her request for extra time.

They **absolutely** refuse to give up on achieving high scores on my English exam.

Diminisher (to tone down or down-toner):

John **almost** gave up studying English.

I **somewhat** agree with you.

Forming an Adverb

An *adverb* can be formed in different ways. Here are a few examples:

1. By adding ***-ly*** to an *adjective*. Examples are:

   absolutely, anxiously, cheerfully, constantly, extremely, hardly, locally, occasionally, perfectly, positively, quickly, rarely, safely, usually, etc.

2. By adding ***-ally*** to an *adjective* ending with ***-ic*** *:*

   academic → academically | athletic → athletically
   automatic → automatically | dramatic → dramatically
   drastic → drastically | fantastic → fantastically

3. By adding ***-ly*** to an *adjective* ending with ***-al*** *:*

   accidental → accidentally | emotional → emotionally
   geographical → geographically | traditional → traditionally
   sentimental → sentimentally | national → nationally

4. If an *adjective* ends in a consonant ***+ -y***, then change ***-y*** to ***-ily*** *:*

   happy → happily | hungry → hungrily
   lazy → lazily | lucky → luckily
   noisy → noisily | speedy → speedily

5. If an *adjective* ends with ***-le***, preceded by a consonant, then change ***-e*** to ***-y*** *:*

   enjoyable → enjoyably | gentle → gently
   fashionable → fashionably | incredible → incredibly
   notable → notably | possible → possibly

6. If an *adjective* ends with ***-le***, preceded by a vowel, then add ***-ly*** *:*

   agile → agilely | sole → solely
   vile → vilely | exception e.g.: whole → wholly

7. If an *adjective* ends with ***-ue***, then change ***-e*** to ***-ly*** *:*

   due → duly | true → truly

Note: There are some *adverbs* that do not end in ***-ly*** and there are some words that end in ***-ly*** that are not *adverbs*. For example:

He drove ***fast***.
She was a *lovely* woman.
I work with many *friendly* people.

❊ Adverb Placement ❊

An *adverb* can be placed in the following manner; however, an *adverb* is never placed between the *verb* and the *object*. Here are some examples:

At the beginning of a sentence, before the *subject:*

adverb + subject + verb (verb phrase) + ...

Unfortunately, we could not (couldn't) go to English language class as planned.

In the middle of a sentence between the *subject* and the *verb:*

subject + adverb + verb (verb phrase) + ...

John **frequently** passed exams with ease.

subject + 'be' verb + adverb + ...

Adam is **continually** showing up unannounced.

At the end of a sentence, after the *verb* or *object:*

subject + verb (verb phrase) + ... + adverb

He talks on his mobile phone **loudly**.

More than one *adverb* in a sentence:

subject + verb (verb phrase) + ... + adverb + ... + adverb

Casper studies English **diligently**, in the library*, **daily***.

It is good practice to limit the use of *adverbs* to one or two per sentence. If more are used, then they should be used sparingly and be thoughtfully placed to maximize their impact, such as:

Consistently, every evening after eating his dinner, John **quietly** studies English **diligently** and **continuously** for hours.

Note: Caution. The overuse of *adverbs* [also true for the overuse of *adjectives*] may overwhelm the recipient and weaken the overall effect of the communication.

❊ Adverb Order ❊

Adverb order is as follows:

1. *degree*   2. *manner*   3. *place*
4. *frequency*   5. *time*

Conjunctive Adverbs

A *conjunctive adverb*, also known as a *connecting adverb*, is used as a connection word to link a deeper relationship between different clauses or sentences. These are words such as:

accordingly	*also*	*anyhow*
consequently	*furthermore*	*however*
moreover	*nevertheless*	*otherwise*
subsequently	*then*	*therefore*

There are several different *conjunctive adverb forms*. Here are a few examples:

1. When a *conjunctive adverb* is used at the beginning of a sentence, a *comma* is placed after the *adverb*, followed by the remaining sentence, such as:

   conjunctive adverb, + main clause

   The actual exam papers were not delivered in time. ***Subsequently,*** there will be no exam today.

2. When a *conjunctive adverb* is used between *two independent clauses*, a *semicolon* is required before the *adverb* with a *comma* following. Examples are:

   main clause; + conjunctive adverb, + main clause

   I want to go and play football**;** ***however,*** I need to study English first.

   I plan to wake up at 06:00**;** ***then,*** if the weather permits, I will go for a 25K run.

3. When a *conjunctive adverb* is placed within a *clause* as an interruption, then *commas* are placed around the *adverb*, to set it off and link the ideas within that and the previous sentence, such as:

   start of main clause, conjunctive adverb, + end of main clause

   The exam is over. I will***, nevertheless,*** attempt to gain permission to take the exam tomorrow.

4. When a *conjunctive adverb* is placed at the end of a *clause* as a conclusion, then a *comma* is placed prior to the *adverb*:

   main clause, + conjunctive adverb

   After studying all night, Rick was too tired to eat breakfast. He did brush his teeth before going to work, ***however***.

5. When a *conjunctive* *adverb* is placed as a weak break or conclusion, then it is unnecessary to use *commas*. Examples are:

> Jack called to say he would be late for work. The manager will **therefore** have to ask others to cover him until he shows up.

> Jack spilled paint all over his suit. Painting the house without coveralls was a mistake **indeed**!

✿ Interrogative Adverbs ✿

An *Interrogative adverb* is usually used at the beginning of a *direct question*.

Note: In formal writing it is best to convert *indirect questions* into *direct questions* as follows:

> Explain to me how you came to that conclusion.
>
> ↓   ↓
>
> How did you come to that conclusion?

The four *interrogative adverbs* are:

how (degree or manner)   *where (place)*   *when (time)*
why (reason)

The interrogative adverb *'how'* can be used in different ways. Here are a few examples:

Used with an *adverb*:

> **How** *quickly* can you come over?

Used with an *adjective*:

> **How** *long* is a piece of string?

Used with *much* and *many:*

> **How** *much* does an education cost?
> **How** *many* students are enrolled in next year's course?

Used to express, in what way, something *did* or *does* form or *happen*:

> **How** *did* you get to school this morning?
> **How** *do* you form a 'how' question?

PART SIX — Prepositions (prep.)

A *preposition* is a word that specifies concepts of *place, motion, direction,* and *time.* A *preposition* usually precedes a *noun, noun phrase* or *pronoun.* The structure is:

... + preposition + noun, noun phrase or pronoun

There are many *prepositions* in the English language. Here is a list of a few:

about	**above**	**across**	**after**
against	along	among	around
as	**at**	**before**	behind
below	**between**	beyond	**by (beside)**
down	**during**	except	**for**
from	**in**	inside	**into**
like	near	of	off
on	onto	opposite	outside
over	**past**	round	**since**
than	through	**to**	toward (s)
under	**until (till)**	up	upon
with	**within**	without	

The most commonly used *prepositions* are *at, in,* and *on.* These *prepositions* are divided into two main groupings, *place* or *time.* Examples of their usage are:

at:

I will be *at* the office all day. (place)

I cannot meet you *at* the moment. (point in time)

in:

I performed *in* Auckland on New Year's day. (place)

John F. Kennedy was assassinated *in* 1963. (point in time)

on:

Put another shrimp *on* the Barbie! (place or position)

Our family tradition is to eat pizza and watch a movie *on* Friday nights. We call this 'pizzovie' night! (point in time)

Note: Further information on *place* and *time prepositions* are discussed within their appropriate sections.

Here are some basic rules when applying *prepositions*. These are:

1. In most cases a *preposition* is followed by a *noun, noun phrase, or pronoun*. Examples are:

   John talked **to** *Jim* about the upcoming exam.

   The bank is **beside** *the language school*.

2. A *noun clause* can be the *object* of a *preposition*, such as:

   There is meaning **in** *what you do*!

3. A *preposition* may include two or more *nouns, noun phrases* or *pronouns* in the same sentence, such as:

   He owns homes **in** *Auckland* and *Seattle*.

4. A *preposition* is never followed by a *verb*. However, if a *verb* is used, it can only be a *gerund*, the **-ing** form of a *verb;* a verb in noun form, such as:

   I am keen **on** *learning* Thai cooking.

5. On occasion, a *preposition* is placed after the *noun, noun phrase* or *pronoun*, such as:

   This is *the student* I was speaking **of**?

6. Sometimes an *adverb* may be the *object*, such as:

   Your suit alterations will be done **by** *then*.

Although a *preposition* is usually placed before the *noun, noun phrase* or *pronoun*, they can also be positioned differently depending on the sentence structure, such as:

Active:

   My wife *has taken good care* **of** me.

Passive:

   The husband *has been well looked* **after**.

Question:

   What are you worrying **for**?

Comparison:

   He's attended more classes **than** I have.

Infinitive:

   These instructions are difficult **to** understand.

✼ Place, Space & Direction: (at, in, on…) ✼

A *place preposition* is used to describe the *place*, *space* or *direction* of a *noun*, *noun phrase* or *pronoun*. The most frequently used *place prepositions* in the English language are: *at, in,* and *on*.

at:

> Used to indicate that something or someone is at a specific place.
>
> …*at* (the) church…   …*at* home…
>
> …*at* the airport…   …*at* the doctor's office…

In:

> Used with a location to indicate a position within, or enclosed by an area or space.
>
> …*in* a town…   …*in* New Zealand…
>
> …*in* the park…   …*in* the room…

on:

> Used to describe a location or position that is physically on top of a place.
>
> …*on* the Sunshine Coast…   …*on* a mountain…
>
> …*on* the table…   … (eggs) *on* toast…

Table 43. Prepositions of Place, Space, Location, or Direction

Point or Place at	Inside a Space in	Surface or Within on
at the bus stop	*in* Vancouver	*on* TV
at the door	*in* a tree	*on* the menu
at the front desk	*in* the building	*on* a train
Prepositions	Categories	Examples
above	higher than	The fog rose *above* the lake.
across	the other side of	Use extreme caution when you walk *across* the road.
below	lower than	The duck dove *below* the water.
by or beside	near or next to	The bank is *beside* the cafe.
from	originate	Aren't Jack and Jill *from* here?
into	to enter	Please go *into* the garage and get my hammer!

✖ Time (at, in, on...) ✖

A *time preposition* is used to define *time*. The following table contains examples for some of the most frequently used *time prepositions* in the English language:

Table 44. Prepositions of Time

Precise Time *at*	Months, Years, etc. *in*	Days, Dates, etc. *on*
at 12 o'clock *at* 3 pm *at* lunchtime *at* bedtime *at* sunrise / sunset *at* the moment Let's meet *at* noon.	*in* December *in* (the) winter *in* the `60s *in* 1963 *in* the last century *in* my lifetime Call me *in* two days.	*on* Monday *on* (*at*) the weekend *on* Tuesdays *on* 21 November, 1963 *on* New Years *on* their birthdays You need to be *on* time.
Prepositions	Categories	Examples
after	later	I prefer that you talk to me *after* work.
before	ahead of previous	Can you meet Ruth and I *before* lunch? There are so many challenges *before* us!
between	separation	I can see you *between* one and two o'clock.
by	by the end of a particular time period	She promised to be here *by* the weekend.
during	position throughout	There should not be any talking *during* exams. He studied mathematics and science *during* the night.
for	duration period	I have not been to a movie *for* a long time. I have been studying *for* almost a year.

Prepositions	Categories	Examples
past	later than	Please meet Lenard and I at half *past* twelve.
since	past to present	The weather has been getting hotter and hotter *since* July.
to	before motion	All textbooks will be issued prior *to* class.
until ('til)	occurrence specified time	They all studied together *until* midnight.
within	period	Jude and I will be there *within* an hour!

❀ Compound or Complex Prepositions ❀

A *compound preposition*, also known as *complex preposition*, is formed with two or more words. This is sometimes referred to as *an idiom phrase*. Here are a few of them:

Two words:

according to	*apart from*	*because of*
due to	*except for*	*instead of*
out of	*prior to*	*where as*

Three or more words:

as far as	*as long as*	*as well as*
by means of	*for lack of*	*in addition to*
in front of	*on behalf of*	*on top of*
with regard to	*with respect to*	*with a view to*

QUOTE:

"When I read some of the rules for speaking and writing the English language correctly, I think any fool can make a rule, and every fool will mind it."

Henry David Thoreau

PART SEVEN — Conjunctions (conj.)

A *conjunction* is used to *link* or *join* phrases, *clauses*, or *two or more words together*, within the same sentence. There are two primary types of *conjunctions*: *coordinating* and *subordinating*, each type utilizing a different subgroup of *correlative* (*double*) *conjunctions*.

�֍ Coordinating Conjunctions �֍

A *coordinating conjunction* is used to *link* or *join phrases, clauses* or *words that are grammatically equal or similar*, in the following manner:

phrase + *coordinating conj.* + phrase

clause + *coordinating conj.* + clause

word + *coordinating conj.* + word

There are seven (7) main *coordinating conjunctions* in the English language. The most commonly used are: *and, or,* and *but.* The other four are*: for, nor, so,* and *yet.* Here are examples of their usage:

and:

Phrases: Would you like a cappuccino *and* biscotto?

Clauses: Students of all ages arrived at school, *and* the daily routine began.

Words: I study both English *and* Japanese.

or:

Phrases: You can wear a suit *or* semi-formal attire.

Clauses: Would you like to drive by car, *or* would you prefer to take a taxi?

Words: I recommend that you visit the UNESCO World Heritage Site Historic Monuments of Ancient Kyoto (Kyoto, Uji and Otsu Cities) once *or* twice.

but:

Phrases: The English language school located in Auckland city is small *but* very credible.

Clauses: Many are called, *but* few are chosen.

The other main *coordinating conjunctions* are:

for:

Mr. John Jones was elected as the president, *for* he was the right person for the job.

---

nor:

I don't believe the Prime-Minister is right, ***nor*** do I think he ever will be.

so:

He has to study for the exam tonight, ***so*** he cannot make it to the party.

yet:

John said he was too sick to go to school, ***yet*** he was well enough to want to go to the movies.

Here are a few rules when using *coordinating conjunctions*:

1. A *coordinating conjunction* will always be placed between the *phrases, clauses* or *words* they link or join.
2. When a *coordinating conjunction* joins *clauses*, a *comma* at the end of the first clause is used for most sentences (see rule #3. exception below):

   I want to become an international business person, so I want to learn the English language.
3. If the *coordinating conjunction* joins *clauses* that are grammatically equal, similar and just a few brief words, a comma is not essential. Furthermore, part of the second clause is omitted, a comma is not required. Examples are:

   He was hungry ***so*** he ate.

   Sophia rushed to work ***and*** (~~she~~) was on time.
4. When the last *coordinating conjunction* used in a list is *'and',* a *comma* is optional:

   My favorite foods are macaroni and cheese, pizza, hot-dogs ***and*** pickles.

Subordinating Conjunctions

A *subordinating conjunction* is used to link or join a *subordinate dependent clause* to a *main clause*, often to compare or show contrast.

There are several *subordinating conjunctions* in the English language. Here are three common examples:

although: They all went paragliding ***although*** no one had experience.

since: My classmates have decided to tour New Zealand together ***since*** no one had any other plans.

until: Please remain seated ***until*** I release you all.

Here are some other *subordinating conjunctions:*

after	*as*	*as if*	*as*
though as long as	*as soon as*	*if*	*if only*
in order that	*in case*	*lest*	*once*
now that	*only if*	*provided that*	*so that*
so long as	*when*	*where*	*whereas*
wherever	*while*	*who*	*why*

Here are a few rules when using *subordinating conjunctions*:

1. A *subordinating conjunction* is placed between a *main clause* and *subordinate dependent clause*. Examples are:

   John attended The University of British Columbia **while** his sister went to Oxford.

   I will go to the shopping mall **once** my mom gives me my allowance.

2. A *subordinate clause* is always dependent on a *main clause*.

3. A *subordinate clause* can often precede an *independent clause:*

   While I was sleeping, my mother cooked dinner.

   Although it was cold outside, Veronica went swimming.

�֍ Correlative or Double Conjunctions �֍

Correlative conjunctions, also known as a *double conjunctions*, are a subgroup of both *coordinating* and *subordinating conjunctions*. They are always used in pairs to *link* or *join* equivalent grammatical elements (parts) in a sentence.

Here are some examples of *coordinating correlative (double) conjunctions:*

both...and... :

Both New Zealand **and** South Africa are rugby nations.

either...or... :

Either Jackson **or** Thompson will win the election.

neither...nor... :

I **neither** like **nor** dislike golf.

not only...but also... :

Jim **not only** scored the winning goal **but** (~~he~~) **also** was selected as the most valuable player.

Here are some examples of *subordinating correlative* (*double*) *conjunctions:*

whether...or... :

Robert has not decided **whether** to go to the soccer **or** stay home and rest.

if...then... :

If it rains tomorrow morning **then** I will need to take my umbrella with me to work.

so...that... :

They were **so** excited **that** their new baseball uniforms had arrived.

Phoney Phonetics *(slightly modified).*

One reason why I cannot spell, although I learned the rules quite well, is that some words like *coup* and *through* sound just like *threw* and *flue* and *who*; when *oo* is never spelled the same, the *duice* becomes a guessing game; and then I ponder over *though*, is it spelled *so*, or *throw*, or *beau*, and *bough* is never *bow*, it's *bow*, I mean the *bow* that sounds like *plow*, and not the *bow* that sounds like *row* - the *row* that is pronounced like *roe*.

I wonder, too, why *rough* and *tough*, that sound the same as *gruff* and *muff*, are spelled like *bough* and *though*, for they are both pronounced a different way.

And why can't I spell *trough* and *cough* the same as I do *scoff* and *golf?*

Why isn't *drought* spelled just like *route*, or *doubt* or *pout* or *sauerkraut?*

When words all sound so much the same to change the spelling seems a shame.

There is no sense - see sound like *cents* - in making such a difference between the sight and sound of words; each spelling rule that undergirds the way a word should look will fail, and often prove to no avail, because exceptions will negate, the truth of what the rule may state; so though I try, I still despair and moan and mutter "It's not fair that I'm held up to ridicule and made to look like such a fool when it's the spelling that's at fault.

Let's call this nonsense to a halt.

Attributed to Vivian Buchan, NEA Journal 1966/67, USA, published in Spelling Progress Bulletin Spring 1966, p6.

PART EIGHT — Interjections (interj.)

An *interjection* is a word used to *express* or *convey* a strong sudden *emotion, sentiment,* or *abrupt remark.* Some *interjections* are:

| disgust | enthusiasm | excitement | surprise |

An *Interjection* is not grammatically related to any other part of a sentence. It is attached to and is usually followed by a *comma* or an *exclamation mark.*

An *Interjections* are not usually used in formal writing, except in *direct quotations, plays,* or *scripts.*

Table 45. Interjections

Interjections	Meanings	Examples
ah	complaint, dislike, joy, pain, pity, pleasure, realization, resignation, surprise	*Ah,* I understand now! *Ah,* that feels good! *Ah!* I don't believe a single word you're saying!
alas	concern, pity, sorrow	*Alas!* The queen has passed.
bugger	imply dissatisfaction	*Bugger,* I lost my keys again!
dear me	distress, pity, surprise, sympathy	*Dear me!* That didn't happen to her did it?
eh	doubt, surprise	*Eh!* I don't believe you!
hello	elation, surprise, wonder	*Hello*---what's going on here? *Hello*---am I glad to see you!
hey	to call attention to, pleasure, surprise, bewilderment	*Hey,* that's great! *Hey!* Get out-ta [sic] here!
hmm or h'm	doubt, hesitation, perplexity, puzzled	*H'm,* I'm not so sure about that!
Jeepers (creepers)	frustration, emotion, surprise	*Jeepers (~ creepers)!* Did that really happen to you?
ooh or oh no	disapprobation, pain, surprise, joy	*Oh no!* I hope it's not true! *Ooh,* is that right?
ouch / ow	dismay, pain	*Ouch!* That really hurts!
ugh	disgust, horror	*Ugh,* this coffee is bitter!

CHAPTER TWO: PUNCTUATION GUIDE

ENGLISH LANGUAGE PUNCTUATION

ACCEPTABLE USAGE

In written English, punctuation marks are used within sentences to remove uncertainty of meaning, or intention. Here is an example of two sentences with the same number of words and same word order, but differing punctuation, giving each sentence a different meaning:

The man ate and sang an hour after his head was cut off.
The man ate and sang; an hour after, his head was cut off.

⌘ Terminating Marks (.) (!) (?) (‽) ⌘

In the current written English language, there are only four *terminating marks* used to end a sentence. These are:

1. A period or full stop (.),
2. An exclamation mark (!),
3. A question mark (?), and
4. An interrobang or interabang (‽).

Period or Full Stop (.)

A *period* (.) [American grammatical terminology] or a *full stop* (.) [British grammatical terminology] is used to end all sentences other than emphasized statements where an *exclamation mark* is used (!), for questions where a *question mark* is used (?), or for emphasized questions where a *interrobang* is used (‽).

A *period* (or *full stop*) goes at the end of a sentence or inside a *closing quotation mark*, such as:

Today is Monday.　　　　He said, "I am hungry."

A *period* (or *full stop*) is used to designate an ordered list when coupled with numbers, the alphabet, or Roman numerals. Examples are:

1.　　　A.　　　a.　　　i.
2.　　　B.　　　b.　　　ii.
3.　　　C.　　　c.　　　iii.

A *period* (or *full stop*) is used to terminate an abbreviation:

Mr.　　　Mrs.　　　Miss.　　　Rev.
etc.　　　e.g.　　　i.e.　　　R.S.V.P.

A *period* (or *full stop*) is used at the end of an indirect quotation, such as:

John asked if it rained yesterday.

A *period* (or *full stop*) is used with some name titles. Examples are:

Dr. Thomas Julian...　　　Cpt. James Kirk...

Exclamation Mark (!)

An *exclamation mark* is used to emphasize a statement, or to express a sudden forceful emotion, plea, or cry. Examples are:

Do not move or I will shoot!　　　Wow!

I said be quiet!　　　Nonsense!

Question Mark (?)

A *question mark* is used to end a direct question that requires a response, such as:

May I borrow a pen?

An enclosed *question mark* (?) is also used to indicate uncertainty or doubt by experts, NOT for use in general practice to indicate a lack of knowledge. An example of the correct usage is as follows:

Joan of Arc, 1412 (?) – 30 May, 1431, is considered a French heroine and Catholic saint.

If a *question mark* is required at the end of a quote that is within *quotation marks*, then the *question mark* is placed inside the *quotation marks*, such as:

John asked, "Where are my keys?"

If a *question mark* is required at the end of a sentence where a quotation is used, then the *question mark* is placed outside the *quotation marks*, such as:

Was John right when he said, "I am the luckiest man alive"?

In a question sentence, which also includes a question within *quotation marks*, use only one *question mark*, as follows:

Did John say, "Where are my keys?"

Note: Grammar rules dictate that only one *terminating mark* can be used in a sentence. However, there is an informal exception to this rule. Grammatically speaking, a exclamatory question *should not* use both a terminating *exclamation mark* (!) and a terminating *question mark* (?) at the same time. The following example is strictly for **informal** purposes:

An *exclamation mark* with a *question mark* at the end of the same sentence; are you kidding !?

The only formal solution to the simultaneous combining of a *terminating exclamation mark* (!) with a *terminating question mark* (?), at the conclusion of a exclamatory question, is the use of an *interrobang* (?).

Interrobang (?)

In formal writing, the *interrobang* [interabang] (?) is used to ask a question emphasizing excitement, disbelief, or to ask a rhetorical question. Examples are:

You said what to her?

She's pregnant again?

✖ Ellipsis (...) ✖

An *ellipsis* (...), three periods in a row, is used to indicate the omission of a word, words, or a sentence or sentences in a quote. Examples are:

"I say to you today, my friends, so even though we face the difficulties of today and tomorrow, ...

I have a dream that one day this nation will rise up and live out the true meaning of its creed...

I have a dream that my four little children will one day live in a nation where they will not be judged by the color of their skin, but by the content of their character.

I have a dream today."

Martin Luther King, Jr.

If an omission occurs after a sentence, the three periods (...) are added after the termination period, such as:

"Twinkle, twinkle, little star. ...like a diamond in the sky."

❀ Comma (,) ❀

A *comma* is used to separate parts of a sentence into logical elements, helping to clarify the meaning of a sentence. A *comma* is generally understood to be a rest in a sentence, a micro-pause, or a place to take a quick shallow breath.

Here are several guidelines for using a *comma* effectively:

Distinguishing Parenthetical Elements

Use a *comma* to separate or distinguish a *parenthetical element* within a sentence. A *parenthetical element,* also referred to as *added information*, is any part of a sentence that can be removed without changing the real meaning of the remaining sentence. Examples are:

John F. Kennedy, the Thirty-fifth President of the United States of America, was assassinated in 1963.

Aung San Suu Kyi, after 15 of the 21 years of house arrest from July 20, 1989 until her release on 13 November 2010, was freed.

Note: *Parentheses* are sometimes used to reduce the importance of *parenthetical information*, such as:

Mr. Jones almost 40-year attendance record (with the exception of one day last June) has been exemplary.

Dashes are sometimes used to emphasize the importance of *parenthetical information*, such as:

Mr. Jones' almost 40-year attendance record—with not one recorded incident of lateness—has been exemplary.

As a general rule, setoff *parenthetical information* with *commas*.

88

Separating Items in a Series

Use a *comma* to separate *words, phrases,* or *clauses* that appear in a series of three or more. The final item should have the *coordinating conjunction 'and'* placed before it. However, in the fourth example below, the word *'and'* is used with words that are inseparable:

1. I love to eat hamburgers, french-fries, onion-rings *and* apple pie.
2. I enjoy playing baseball at the park, taking long walks on the beech, hiking in the summer *and* swimming in the ocean.
3. My favorite sports are rugby, golf, soccer, yachting *and* fishing.
4. My favorite foods are macaroni *and* cheese *and* fish *and* chips.

The *'and'* between the word *'macaroni'* and the word *'cheese'*, is placed to facilitate a link between two inseparable words, within the context of *'macaroni and cheese'* [to reflect one item or entity]. If macaroni, cheese, pizza, hot-dogs and pickles were expressed, then (in contrast) the meaning would change. In the forth example, there are two items, and in the example inserted within this paragraph, there are five.

Serial (Oxford or Harvard) Comma

Use a *Serial Comma,* also known as a *Oxford, Harvard* or *Series Comma,* before the word *'and'* or *'or'* at the end of a sentence that contains a series of separate words, phrases, or clauses that appear in a series of three or more, such as:

My favorite hobbies are hiking, camping, fishing, and hunting.

Note: There is ongoing debate over the use of such a *comma.* Generally speaking, the *coordinating conjunctions 'and'* or *'or'* replace a *comma,* so some 'grammar experts' claim that the use of a *comma* coupled with the word *'and'* or *'or'* is redundant; however, if an *Serial Comma* can be used to prevent confusion, then common sense should prevail.

Introductory Phrase or Adverb Clause

Use a *comma* after an *introductory phrase* or *adverb clause* that precedes the subject of the sentence. Examples are:

An Introductory phrase:

Staring up at Mount Everest for the first time, he suddenly realized how insignificant he was.

An Adverb clause:

If the next two nights are sellouts, the concert schedule will be extended.

Setting Off Interruptions

Use a *pair of commas* to set off *words, phrases,* or *clauses* that interrupt a sentence. Examples are:

Success, for the most part, is the application of a positive attitude.

The Weather channel stated that the weather this week, I hope, will be absolutely fantastic.

However, be careful not to directly affect the essential meaning of the sentence by adding these elements.

Separating Dialog and Non-dialog Text

A *hyphen,* or *hyphens,* are used to *separate dialog* and *non-dialog text,* using introductory words. Here are a few of many, which can take different speech forms:

ask	*assert*	*boast*	*charge*
claim	*comment*	*continue*	*debate*
demand	*exclaim*	*hint*	*inform*
plead	*protest*	*said*	*write*

When a quote follows an introductory word, the *comma* is placed after the introductory word, a space is added, then an open *quotation mark* used, followed by the quote with the first letter capitalized; unless an *ellipsis* (...) is used to start the quote. Examples are:

Martin Luther King, Jr. has become famous for the words in a speech he gave in which he said, "I have a dream today."

or

Martin Luther King, Jr. expressed hope when he said, "...my four little children will one day live in a nation where they will not be judged by the color of their skin... I have a dream today."

When an introductory word follows a quote, the *comma* is placed after the final word of the quote, directly followed by a closing *quotation mark,* a space, and then the introductory word, such as:

"I have a dream today," said Martin Luther King, Jr. as he addressed the masses.

When introductory words are within a quote the correct punctuation will be as follows:

"...my four little children," said Martin Luther King, Jr., "will one day live in a nation where they will not be judged by the color of their skin... I have a dream today."

When an introductory and non-quote words are used before and after the quote the correct punctuation will be as follows:

Martin Luther King, Jr. said, "I have a dream today," as crowds of people listened.

Before a Coordinating Conjunction

A *coordinating conjunction* provides a connection between two similarly constructed and / or syntactically equal *words, phrases,* or *clauses* within a sentence. Examples of such words are:

| for | and | nor | but |
| or | yet | so | |

A *comma,* followed by one space, is placed before the *coordinating conjunction.* Examples are:

Jane screamed loudly, **for** she could no longer tolerate the pain.

To avoid being caught by police, Tom agreed to take the first watch, **and** Jim promised to relieve him within an hour.

Tom will never attempt bungee-jump, **nor** will he sky drive.

Jane dislikes running and swimming, **but** loves hiking.

I have a strong feeling it will rain today, **or** maybe it won't.

Jane is an extremely hyperactive individual, **yet** she will spend several hours watching a professional chess match.

Jim is unable to come to the party, **so** let's take the party to him.

The use of a *comma* before the *coordinating conjunction 'and'* or *'or'* is generally accepted as optional (see Serial Comma).

Separating Date Elements

Use a *comma* to separate the date from the year (American written dates only). Examples are:

January 26, 2012 (American)
26 January 2012 (British)

Use a *comma* to separate the day from the date. Examples are:

Tuesday, June 12, 2012 (American)

Tuesday, 12 June 2012 (British)

Within a sentence, use a *comma* on both sides of the year in a full American date (day, month with date, and year) and only on the right side of the year for a British date (day, date with month and year). Examples are:

On Friday, March 29, 2012, my Mom will have a birthday. (American)

On Friday, 29 March 2012, my Mom will have a birthday. (British)

Note: A *comma* is not used for two date elements, such as:

J. F. Kennedy's assassination in November 1963 is a moment in time many Americans are unwilling to forget.

Separating Number Elements

Use a *comma* in numbers of more than three digits, from right to left, as a thousands' separator. Examples are:

He had $12,527 in his bank account.

There were 57,653 people at the Rugby World Cup final.

Common exceptions include, but are not limited to this list:

1. Some countries (currency may differ),

2. Only use a *comma* in years of five digits or more, such as in 12,500 BC,

3. Street numbers may not use a *comma*, and

4. Page numbers.

Note: There may be many others. Self-study will be necessary.

Use a *comma* to separate related written measurements, such as:

The heavyweight boxer was six-feet, two-inches tall, and at weigh-in 180 pounds, 6 ounces.

Use a *comma* to separate elements in a play, such as:

Act III, Scene II, "Friends, Romans, countrymen, lend me your ears; I come to bury Caesar, not to praise him."

Within Names, Places, and Addresses

Use a *comma* to separate people's names and their academic degrees, such as:

> David Alexandra, MD, will speak at the conference.

Use a *comma* between a name when a surname comes before a first, such as:

> Kennedy, John F. was assassinated in November 1963.

Use a *comma* to separate place names with the smallest unit first, such as:

> John lives on 12 Oaks Road, New York city, New York State, USA.
>
> *or, in a mailing address:*
>
> John Jones
> 2347A 12 Oaks Road,
> New York, N.Y.,
> U.S.A.

Colon (:)

A *colon* is usually used in conjunction with the preceding word and words. Examples are:

> as follows: are: as: is:

A *colon* is used prior to a numbered list, a summarized list (within a sentence), or an indirect quote. Examples are:

A list:

> My favorite pets are:
>
> 1. dogs,
> 2. horses, and
> 3. snakes.

A summarized list:

> Before we depart we must achieve the following: catch the shark, tag it, and then release it unharmed.

An indirect quote:

> ...as Khalil Gibran wrote: and in much of your talking, thinking is half murdered.

A *colon* can be used to dramatically emphasize a single word or phrase, such as:

There was only one choice left to make: resign!

A *colon* is used to divide a primary division from a secondary division. Examples are:

Religious books:

The shortest verse in the King James version of the Christian Holy Bible is, John 11:35 "Jesus Wept."

In the Holy Quran 55:64 " مدهامتان ‏."

Time:

| 09:15 | 12:25 | 18:30 |

The use of *capitalization* or *lower-case* after a *colon* varies. In British English the word following the *colon* is in lower-case unless it is a proper noun, an acronym, or if it is normally *capitalized* for some other reason. In American English the word following a *colon* is *capitalized* only if it begins an *independent clause*.

�֎ Semicolon (;) �֎

The *semicolon* is used to join an *independent clause* that is closely related in meaning. Examples are:

Reducing fat in your diet will decrease the chances of heart disease; regular exercise is also important.

Note: Generally speaking, use a *semicolon* only where a period could also be used.

The *semicolon* is also used to separate word groupings, such as:

The New Zealand All-blacks battled the South African Springbok for 80-minutes of pure rugby, all players were tired, bruised, and exhausted; it was pride, passion, and the reward of victory that kept them all going.

Dash (—) or (--), and Swung Dash (~)

A *dash* is used to *emphasize, support,* or *explain,* and / or to *note a sharp change in thought.* Examples are:

Emphasis:

The concert was exciting—a fantastic show.

She is beautiful--a knockout.

Support or explain:

The Color Purple (1985) directed by Steven Spielberg—the first of several movies staring Oprah Gail Winfrey—is a classic.

President J. F. Kennedy--assassinated on November 22, 1963 (aged 46)--was sworn in as the 35th President of The United States of America at noon on January 20, 1961.

A sharp change in thought:

I'm sure Janet will go to the movies with you—I don't think she would say no.

A *dash* can also be used to express *hesitation* when writing, usually preceded with a word that reflects that a person is pondering the next idea. Examples are:

I mean:

I'm not sure if I want to go fishing, I mean—what if a big storm rolls in and we can't get back to shore?

I think:

Let's drive all night to Vegas. I think—no—I know we can make it before daylight, if we rotate drivers.

Maybe:

She said she would be here at 5 o'clock—maybe something has happened to her.

Um or ah:

John: Why are you late for work?

Jane: Um—Ah—I was kidnapped by aliens.

A *swung dash* is used to separate alternatives or indicate approximates. In dictionaries, a *swung dash* is frequently used to substitute a term being defined. For example, the word *'henceforth'* [(adv.) from this time forth; from now on], might be substituted with a *swung dash* in the following way:

"~ he will be known as *The Duke of York.*"

Hyphen (-)

Between Compound Words

A *hyphen* is used between the individual parts of *compound words* to act as one idea. Examples are:

Between two *nouns:*

Christopher Neil, Bob Dylan, Amy Winehouse, and Lady Gaga are or were *singer-songwriters*.

You can buy milk at the *corner-store*.

Between two *adjectives* placed before a *noun:*

It is much more expensive to buy a *first-class* ticket.

He has a *care-free* attitude.

Between two *verbs:*

You need to *dry-clean* your pants before the next meeting.

The plane had to *crash-land*.

Between an *adjective* and a *noun:*

I bought a *loose-leaf* binder at the shop.

I attended an *open-air* concert.

Between a *noun* and a *verb:*

It was *back-breaking* work.

I was *hand-picked* to attend the seminar.

Two Words Linked by a Preposition

Sometimes two or more words are linked by *prepositions* with *hyphens*. Examples are:

She is my *sister-in-law*.

He is really a *down-to-earth* person.

It is true *as-a-matter-of-fact*!

I had the *right-of-way*.

Spelt Numbers and Cardinals

A *hyphen* is used between *spelt numbers* and also between a *spelt number* and a *cardinal*. Examples are:

I have collected *twenty-three vintage-cars over thirty-three* years.

Less than *one-forth* of homes are adequately insulated.

Words with a Prefix

A *hyphen* is used after a *prefix*. Examples are:

The *prefix 'anti-'* expresses opposition to (or being against) the root word that adjoins it:

> I operated an ***anti***-*aircraft* gun during WWII.

> The ***anti***-*crime* unit hit with force.

The *prefix 'by-'* suggests that something has two, is doubled, or repeated or is secondary to the root word and is sometimes *hyphenated*. Examples are:

> A ***by***-*product* of corn is organic fuel.

> The city's ***by***-*law* states no dogs on any beach.

But not as in:

> The city bypass is almost complete.

> Let bygones be bygones.

The *prefix 'co-'* is used if the root word, usually a *verb* or it's *noun* derivative, begins with the letter **'o'** or with a *noun* to denote joint participation. Examples are:

> The charity held a ***co***-*operative* fundraiser.

> I need a ***co***-*ordinator* for the International Student Services position filled by Wednesday next week.

> *or*

> My husband is a great ***co***-driver on long journeys.

> It is rare that a ***co***-*star* is paid more than the star.

The *prefix 'counter-'* is used *'speak out'* or to *'act in opposition to'* something. Examples are:

> The 10th Mountain Division planned a ***counter***-*attack*.

> Arguing with a deadline looming can be ***counter***-*productive*.

But not as in:

> The painting is a counterfeit.

> It was necessary to counteract their action.

The *prefix 'ex-'* is used to expresses a former state to the root word. Examples are:

> He is my ***ex***-*husband*.

> Should I hire an ***ex***-*convict*?

The *prefix 'in-'* expresses an inclusion within *space, time* or *circumstances*. In most cases a hyphen is not used, but is used as in these examples:

I want to hire *in-house*.

I will have surgery at the *in-patient* clinic.

But not as in:

The lovers were **in**separable. Are they **in**sane?

The *prefix 'non-'* reflects that there is a *'lesser value to'* or *'a lack of'* in relation to the root word. Examples are:

I prefer **non**-*alcoholic* drinks.

All **non**-*essential* workers were asked to go home.

The *prefix 're-'* (to do again) is used if the root word begins with the letter *'e'*. Examples are:

It was necessary to **re**-*edit* the book prior to publishing after new information was found.

I had to **re**-*establish* the restaurant after years of neglect.

The *prefix 're-'* is also used when forming a compound word, Not using a hyphen may change the words meaning, as in:

recover	**re**-*cover*	reform	**re**-*form*
react	**re**-*act*		

Note: When a consonant or the letter *'a'* follows the prefix, a hyphen is not usually used, as in these two examples:

rebound   rearrange

The *prefix 'self-'* is used to show that a person is acting of one's own accord, such as:

I have always been **self**-*employed*.

I believe that I am a **self**-*motivated* individual.

Words with a Suffix

A *hyphen* is used after *suffixes*. Examples are:

-all	-away	-back	-by
-down	-in	-off	-on
-out	-over	-up	and others.

Here are a few examples of the above *suffixes*:

be-**all** and end-**all**	give-**away**	out-**back**	kick-**off**
stand-**by**	shut-**down**	check-**in**	knock-**out**
make-**over**	clean-**up**	try-**on**	

Apostrophe (')

Omission of Letters in a Contraction

Use an *apostrophe* to replace letters omitted in a shortened form of a word or group of words called a *contraction*:

Table 46. Omitting of Letters in a Contraction (Sample List)

Word	Contr.	Word	Contr.	Word	Contr.
are not	aren't	cannot	can't	did not	didn't
do not	don't	had not	hadn't	has not	hasn't
have not	haven't	I am	I'm	I have	I've
is not	isn't	let us	let's	they are	they're
we have	we've	will not	won't	you are	you're
he had he would	he'd	he will he shall	he'll	I had I would	I'd
she had she would	she'd	they will they shall	they'll	what is what has	what's

The use of a *contraction* is related to whom the writing is directed. In formal writing, such as: *memos, casual letters, emails*, or *blogs,* etc., *contractions* are acceptable. With formal writing, such as: for *academic* or *business purposes*, etc., then tone becomes more important and the use of *contractions* less likely.

With Possessive Nouns

See the section on *possessive nouns.*

Parentheses ( ) and Brackets [ ]

Parentheses ( )

Use *parentheses* to interject relevant text within other text to further clarify, inform or qualify the preceding idea. Text within *parentheses* shows less importance, such as:

He finally showed up (although we had other things to occupy our time), so we cheerfully continued with the presentation, without further delay.

Note:

1. Normal punctuation is used within *parentheses* if a full sentence is written (most of the time this will be a *comma*, *period*, or a *full-stop*).

2. *Dashes* should be used if emphasis is needed, such as:

> He finally showed up—even though we had been waiting for more than three hours, frustrated and annoyed—we continued reluctantly.

Use *parentheses* to inject an option within text:

> He finally showed up (bad traffic I reckon) so we continued with the presentation.

Use *parentheses* to note the year of a particular publication and also any page number within that publication that a reference was taken. The full reference would need to be listed at the conclusion of the main text under the title 'References.' Here is an example:

Within Text (APA Formatting):

> *Martin Luther King Jr., (1958) was an American Baptist Minister, an activist and a prominent leader in the American civil rights movement. He said that, "Men often hate each other because they fear each other; they fear each other because they don't know each other; they don't know each other because they cannot communicate; they cannot communicate because they are separated." (p. 20)*

Reference (s):

> King Jr., M. L. (1958). *Stride toward freedom: The Montgomery story.* New York, NY: Harper.

Use *parentheses* within a sentence to enclose numbers or letters used for listed items, such as:

> We require a Marketing Manager to fill the position who can (1) protect our brand, (2) increase cash-flow by 15%, (3) have vision, and (4) blend into the companies culture seamlessly.

Use *partial* or *full parentheses* for lists using numbers and letters, as in:

a) salt	b) pepper	c) sugar	d) flour
(a) salt	(b) pepper	(c) sugar	(d) flour

Brackets [ ]

Use *brackets* as insertion marks to inject additional information, clarify [reduce uncertainty], reinforce, criticize or explain, a particular word or phrase, which would not normally be part of the sentence, such as:

> I observed John as he approached the panel. He wore a bright red [magenta] suit to the interview. It was a good thing that I was wearing my sunglasses!

Use *brackets* to inject the writer's opinion, which may or may not be in context, such as:

> John Lennon was murdered [or assassinated] on 8 December, 1980 (aged 40), in New York city, United States of America.

Use *brackets* when inserting comments or information that is not part of the original quote and / or may not be essential, such as:

> "And so, my fellow Americans: ask not what your country can do for you - ask what you can do for your country. My fellow citizens of the world: ask not what America will do for you, but what together we can do for the freedom of man [in a completely non-chauvinist form of the word *'man'*]."

Use *brackets* for editorial information, such as:

> To enclose parenthetical information that appears inside other parenthetical information. For example:

>> The director / producer (Peter Jackson, [born 31 October, 1961]), made famous by the trilogy 'Lord of the Rings,' also made many other hit movies.

>> Peter Jackson (My friend of five years [the sale's clerk, not the celebrity movie producer from New Zealand], and the man I would trust with my life) is coming to dinner.

Use *brackets* around the *Latin adverb 'sic'* [sic] to indicate and highlight a recognized misspelled word or minor error in a quotation:

> "There were eigt [sic] workers who were found alive at the building site accident. Twenty-two were not so lucky."

QUOTE:

"It is not the answer that enlightens, but the question."

Eugene Ionesco

✖ Double and Single Quotation Marks (" ") (' ') ✖

Use *double quotation marks* to encapsulate a direct quote, such as:

She asked, "John, what time will you leave for the concert?"

However, a quotation is not needed with the following example:

She asked John what time he would leave for the concert.*

*Note: the two example sentences above differ in meaning.

Use *single quotation marks* to encapsulate a quote within a *double quotation-marked direct quote*, such as:

John said, "Jim asked, 'What time will you leave for the concert?'"

Use *single quotation marks* to set off a nickname or to show shortened versions of names. Examples are:

Dimetrios Georgios Synodinos (1918 to 1996), also known as 'Jimmy the Greek' Snyder, was an American sports commentator.

'Christopher Neil' [Christopher Neil Linton] is a New Zealand born musician who released two pop-ballads in British Columbia, Canada (1982), with limited success. His single was also released in New Zealand, the rest of Canada, and also The United States.

Almost always, place a *period* or *comma* inside a closing *double* and *single quotation mark*. Examples are:

The crosswalk lights changed from "Walk," to "Don't Walk," to "Walk" several times in a relatively short period-of-time.

John said, "I found my keys."

✖ Capital Letters (Aa Bb Cc) ✖

Use *capital letters*, also known as *'Upper Case'* letters in the following situations:

1. The first word of any sentence.
2. All proper nouns. Here are several examples:

   Title and / or name of a person: *Governor Lee, SGT. Kay, ...*
   Places: *The United Kingdom, Vancouver B.C., Canada, ...*
   Territories: *Virgin Islands, Victoria, Northern Territories, ...*
   Regions: *Kanagawa Prefecture in Japan, East Africa, ...*
   Provinces: *Nova Scotia, The Western Cape, Limerick, ...*

States: *Georgia, Idaho, New Jersey, ...*

Parishes: *Surrey, Essex, North Yorkshire, Lancashire, ...*

Districts: *Ashbourne District, District of Pi Pizzeria, ...*

Things: *Queen Mary II* (Ship), *Bismarck, Apollo 13, ...*

Days of the week: *Monday to Sunday.*

Months of the year: *January to December.*

Holidays: *Thanksgiving, Children's Day, Al Hijra, ...*

Festivals: *Lunar New Year Festival or Maudi Graw, ...*

3. A person's title when it precedes their name, but not capitalized when the title is acting as a description following the name, such as:

   Sergeant Jones is a hero.

   > *not*

   James Jones, a sergeant, is a hero.

4. An official company or organization's title and / or its abbreviation. Examples are:

   The New Zealand Qualification's Authority or NZQA

   The Federal Bureau of Investigation or FBI

   The Bureau, or FBI, was fast approaching its 50th anniversary.

5. The first and last words of a publication title, but not function words within a title, such as: *a, an, as, but, if, or, nor* and *the* or prepositions, regardless of their length. Examples are:

   The Power of the Platform: Speakers on Purpose.

   Chicken Soup for the Soul.

   Capitalize other words within a title, including the short verb forms *are, be,* and *is, etc.* Examples are:

   Men Are from Mars, Women Are from Venus.

   What Color Is Your Parachute?

6. Course names. Examples are:

   Reflecting on Professional Practice . . . . Algebra 101

   Leading in Diverse Cultures . . . . Intro. to Art

7. The first word of a salutation or complementary clause:

Dear John	To whom it may concern
Sincerely yours	With kindness

8. Cardinal points when they refer to specific regions, but not when they refer to directions, as in:

   I live on the North Island of New Zealand.

   or *'north'* un-capitalized, as in:

   I will travel up north today.

Inconspicuous Stressing: *Italics*

To *emphasize* a word or phrase and avoid the **'blackness effect'** on a page [not wanting text to jump out from other words in a conspicuous manner], styles are used such as *italics* or *oblique* scripts.

Italics are normally used for words and phrases in the following manner:

1. To *emphasize* words and phrases. Examples are:

   Kyoto, Japan boasts 17 properties listed as world heritage sites. The *old* temples and shrines on these properties, with their intricate gardens, are breathtakingly beautiful.

   Do not use a *CAPITALIZED WORD* or *WORDS* for emphasis; use ***bold italics*** instead.

2. The title of complete works. Examples are:

   Have you read the book called *The Power of the Platform*?

   Do you subscribe to *Time* magazine?

   Did you see the cover story in the *New York Times* newspaper?

   I am going to play *Fiddler on the Roof* this Sunday.

   Isn't *Gone with the Wind* a wonderful classic movie?

   I always watch the *20 / 20* investigative reporting show on the TV each week.

   Have you seen the *Mona Lisa* [also known as *La Gioconda* or *La Joconde*] painted by Leonardo di ser Piero da Vinci?

   John Lennon released the album *Imagine* in 1971.

3. Names of aircraft, ships, and trains. Examples are:

   The *Hughes Aircraft Company* was responsible for designing and building the Hughes H-4 Hercules, also known as the *Spruce Goose*.

The *Bismarck* was a famous German battleship during the Second World War.

The New Zealand Railways North Island cross-country train, called the *Blue Streak,* operated between 1968 and 1977.

4. Foreign words used in an English sentence, such as:

   After visiting the many children around Paris, I said goodbye to France, no, *Au revoir les enfants* [French for 'Goodbye, Children'].

5. Words and letters discussed as words and letters within a sentence, such as:

   The ***'-y'*** in a singular noun form is changed to ***'-ie'*** in most cases, such as: lady to ladies or baby to babies.

Bolding

Bold fonts are used to increase contrast with *emphasis* between main text and body text: Headings, subheadings and / or titles, or to highlight important sections or points. ***Bold fonts*** should be used sparingly!

Here is an example taken from a personal development book called, *How to Make People Like You in 90 Seconds*, by Nicholas Boothman (2000).

Heading: **5. Actions Do Speak Louder Than Words**

Subheading: **Body Language**

Section Title: ***Flirting***

Emphasized Text (indented and bold italics are used):

"Appearing sincere, or congruent, is a key ingredient for building the trust that opens the door to likeability and rapport.

Make sure that your words, your tonality and your gestures are all saying the same thing. Be on the lookout for incongruity in others. Notice how it makes you feel.

We've all seen those old movies where a couple of people are driving along in a car, and they're rocking the steering wheel even though the background..." (p. 60)

Bullet Points

Use *bullet points* to highlight important information in an unnumbered list, so that the reader can identify key points of fact quickly. Here are some basic points to consider when using *bullet points*:

1. The sentence introducing a *bulleted list* should always end with a colon (:).
2. If the text after the *bullet point* is a complete sentence, it must begin with a capital letter. Ending punctuation is good practice, but not essential, such as:
    - The first letter in a sentence must be capitalized.
    - All proper nouns must be capitalized.
3. If the text is not a full sentence, a *capital letter* is optional; styling is the main consideration when considering *capital letters* in this situation. Ending punctuation is not required. Here are examples:
    - the first letter in a sentence
    - proper nouns
4. Begin each *bullet point* or sentence using the same word class (or part of speech) such as the use of action verbs. Also keep the tense or future time usage consistent. For example:
    - **teach** five lessons a day for a week
    - **learn** three new concepts each month
    - **develop** two new lessons each quarter
5. *Bullet points* are used to summarize main points, should be visually appealing, and easy to read. For greater impact keep the sentences or text short and use bulleted lists sparingly.

QUOTE:

"Nostalgia is like a grammar lesson; you find the present tense and the past perfect."

Owens Lee Pomeroy

CHAPTER THREE: WRITING GUIDE

THE WRITING PROCESS

COMPOSITION and ACADEMIC WRITING

Many composition and academic writing classes emphasize that writing is an organized process. One such process is to divide the work into five main stages, with these main stages often subdivided into more discrete steps or parts. The main stages are:

1. Prewriting,
2. Drafting,
3. Revising and Editing,
4. Proofing, and
5. Submitting or Publishing.

Prewriting: Organizing Thoughts

Elements of *prewriting* may include planning, researching, outlining, diagramming, storyboarding or clustering. Prior to writing, an opportunity to ask directed questions could be given:

1. What is the purpose for creating the composition / manuscript?
2. Who is the target audience, and will the topic be of high interest, or value to them?
3. What is the specific *'point of difference'* that makes the story, information, or message more captivating or of higher value than other writers of similar material?

Try to get a writer to compose for a purpose other than to please the teacher, solely focused on achieving a good grade, or to satisfy a course requirement. If the writer writes with purpose, they are more likely to become self-motivated rather than pressure driven.

Choose a topic relevant to the writer's real life. In fact, have them directed toward the goal of reading the composition to a person or group of their choosing at completion. When the appropriate support is given, this simple dynamic will create motivation, purpose and a higher quality of work.

Get the writer to conduct real research on their topic. Task them to gather five to ten facts to support their idea, either by using the school or local library, or the internet. Get the writer to document the source of the information that they have gathered, such as: URL links to music videos, photos, or web sites. They should also reference the author, date of publication for books and magazines, or any other sources used [A.P.A. or Harvard Formatting]. It is also very important to educate the writer about plagiarism and copyright infringement.

Once the writer has researched and gathered information, a circle discussion can be held where all writers can 'show-and-tell' their topic to the group. This generates teacher-peer feedback, useful information to assist the writer as they organize their topic toward the next step, a mind map.

Mind Mapping

A *mind or bubble map*—also called a *spider diagram*, or an *idea clustering*—is a graphical method of planning ideas, to present a vision in an organized sequential way. These organizational maps generally take on a hierarchical, tree branch, or spider-legs format of connected ideas, with these ideas branching off into subsections. A mind map can be used for a single paragraph or to create a composition or essay.

There are two main reasons to create and use a *mind map*. They are:

1. to organize initial thoughts, and
2. to serve as a cue, to trigger memory while writing.

The mind map used for this book was a spider-diagram (see Diagram 1.) and is shown here as an example; however, it is important to understand that the mapping process used may differ from one individual to another, so adapting an individual style that works best may be necessary:

Step one: The main idea; working title or concept (the body).

A small rounded rectangle was drawn in the center of the page, representing the main theme or concept for the spider diagram (the body). The center rectangle was vertically split in half. In the right-half segment the words *Grammar Reference* was written. In the left-half segment the words *Teacher's Guide* was written.

Step two: Breaking the main themes down into manageable main ideas. In the book's example, this was the chapters. Seven primary spider-legs representing each chapter and the appendix [initially labeled '...Resources'], were drawn from the center rectangle; labeled with the working chapter's titles:

> Chapter One: English Words.
>
> Chapter Two: Punctuation, and so on.

Step three: Secondary Spider-legs.

Secondary spider-legs (curved lines) were then draw from each primary spider-leg. These secondary spider-legs represent each of the chapter's sub-sections. In the case of *Chapter One: English Words*, the sub-section titles were:

1. Nouns	2. Adjectives
3. Pronouns	4. Verbs
5. Adverbs	6. Prepositions
7. Conjunctions	8. Interjections

Step four: Breaking it down into deeper subsections (the toes).

The sections were broken down into sub-sections, such as:

> *Conjunctions* were broken down into three categories:
>
> 1. Coordinating,
> 2. Subordinating, and
> 3. Correlative or Double.

Diagram 1. Spider Diagram used for this Book

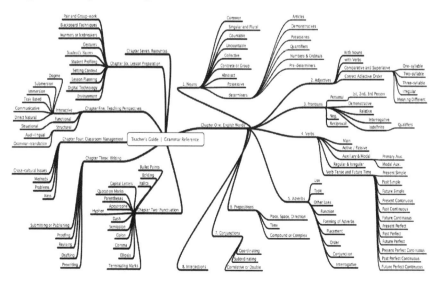

Diagram 2. Bubble Map

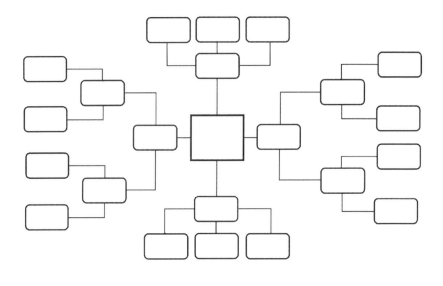

❀ **Drafting** ❀

After the prewriting process has been achieved, the next process is to write a first draft. This process involves developing an overall holistic text, focused *'on topic'*, toward a specific word or page length.

Elements of a first draft may include:

1. identifying the central idea, argument, or theme,

2. converting mind map ideas into cohesively organized paragraphs that reflect the central idea, argument, or theme,

3. organizing supporting or opposing scientific or intellectual research, surveys, or other data, in the appropriate places, throughout the composition,

4. creating an effect flow from one idea to the next, by using transitional sentences.

The following section can be used for instruction on how to create a single paragraph, as an assignment, or to create multiple paragraphs for a larger writing project, such as a composition or essay, using transitional sentences to do so (see *Transitional Sentence*).

Paragraph Construction

The purpose of forming text into paragraphs is to express multiple points in an organized way. Each paragraph should express a single point, an idea, or an opinion that maintains sentence unity and coherence.

Each new paragraph should introduce a new topic, or be used to change speakers when writing dialogue. Toward the conclusion of the presentation a paragraph or paragraphs provide a summary of the combined topics with a conclusion, or ending.

Although there are no specific rules on paragraph length, it is advised that paragraphs should not be so long that the drawn-out writing or dialog is likely to tire or overwhelm the reader. It is accepted practice to break a lengthy paragraph of one topic into related multiple topic specific paragraphs, to provide reading ease.

A paragraph is organized and expressed with three unified elements. These elements are:

1. A Topic Sentence,
2. Supporting Sentence (s), and
3. Concluding Sentence (s).

Topic Sentence

A *topic sentence* is a single sentence that introduces or states the topic for that paragraph, or if needed to introduce multiple paragraphs specific to that topic. This single sentence reflects the main idea, point, or opinion to be developed or explained. This sentence should contain a strong verb, assisting in creating a statement that stands out from other sentences in the paragraph or related paragraphs that follow.

This is an example of a topic sentence:

Special needs students require additional support if they are to succeed academically and emotionally.

Each subsequent sentence in the same paragraph, or multiple paragraphs specific to that topic should be relevant; providing unity throughout the paragraph or multiple paragraphs.

Supporting Sentences

Supporting sentences are one or more sentences that strengthen the preceding *topic sentence*. Supporting sentences often provide the evidence to support the topic, such as: facts, statistics, examples, logical reasoning, quotes or a reference or references of other intellectual contributors on the topic.

This is an example of a supporting sentence:

In fact, studies have shown that special needs students who are correctly identified and supported consistently achieve higher academic scores on tests. Clinical analysis further suggests that this support greatly improves self-confidence and self-worth, providing students with the increased ability to focus more intensely on academic materials.

Concluding Sentences

Concluding sentences are one or more sentences that consolidate the paragraph's or paragraphs' supporting sentences before transitioning to the next topic and subsequent paragraphs.

This is an example of a concluding sentence:

Appropriate academic and emotional support are clearly required for special needs students to allow the best possible chances of success in their pursuit of studies and a happier life.

Sentence Unity and Coherence

Sentence unity and coherence can be achieved by using transition words or phrases. Transition words and phrases can be used for many situations. Here are several examples:

For opening an initial paragraph, or for general use:

generally speaking	unquestionably	admittedly
nobody denies	assuredly	certainly
granted (that)	no doubt	obviously
of course	to be sure	undoubtedly
in general	at this level	in this situation

For continuing a common line of reasoning:

consequently	clearly, then	and furthermore
moreover	besides that	additionally
in addition	because	in the same way
following this	further	also
it is easy to see that	pursuing this further	in light of

To change the line of reasoning:

on the other hand	on the contrary	in contrast
nevertheless	but, *or* yet	however
in spite of	despite	even though

For comparison:

| similarly | comparable | likewise |
| in the same way | just as | so too |

For contrast:

however	notwithstanding	despite
on the other hand	rather	even so
on the contrary	in contrast	nonetheless
at the same time	though this may be	nevertheless
instead	alternatively	otherwise
still	but	and yet

For summary or for emphasis:

in short	in brief	in fact
in truth	in reality	in any event
in other words	in summary	indeed
in general	of course	remarkably
assuredly	definitely	certainly
as I stated	clearly	importantly
without doubt	generally	after all
I hope	naturally	it seems
on the whole		

For the final points of a paragraph or essay:

| finally | lastly | in closing |

To chronologically adjoin multiple paragraphs which link to the same topic sentence:

first, ...	second, ...	third, ...
generally	furthermore	finally
as well	also	lastly
in the first place	pursuing this further	basically
to be sure	additionally	similarly
just in the same way		

To signal a conclusion:

therefore	this concludes	hence
in final analysis	in conclusion	indeed
in the end	in final consideration	

To restate a point within a paragraph in another way or in a more exacting way:

in other words	to reinforce this idea	specifically
that is to say	or	

Sequence or time:

subsequently	afterwards	later
as soon as	after	before
at first	at last	at length
at that time	presently	recently
long	finally	as of late
in the first place	meanwhile	immediately
first, ...	second, ...	third, ...
in the future	in the meantime	in the past
soon	then	thereafter
eventually	currently	now
earlier	next	

Misused Words

Homonym, Homograph, Homophone

A *homonym* is two or more words having different meanings, but the same spelling and pronunciation, such as: race (n.) [a competition between runners] and race (n.) [a group of people sharing distinct physical characteristics or culture, history and language].

A *homograph* is two or more words having different meanings, the same spelling, but not necessarily pronounced the same, such as: bow (v.) [bend the head or upper part of the body as a sign of respect, greeting, or shame] and bow (n.) [bent or curved in shape].

A *homophone* is two or more words having different meanings and spelling, but the same pronunciation, such as: knew (v.) [past tense of the word 'know' - to understand a person, place or thing, etc.], and new (adj.) [not existing before, freshly or recently produced, introduced or discovered, etc.].

Table 47. Homonym, Homograph, and Homophone Definitions

Term	Meaning	Spelling	Pronunciation
Homonym	different	the same	the same
Homograph	different	the same	different
Homophone	different	different	the same

Common mistakes in English usage are often made not only by those that are learning the English language (speakers of other languages), but also by native speakers.

The most important thing to remember about any language is that the underlining purpose for language is to communicate a message. If a message is being passed on from one person to another, through spoken communication with a few common mistakes, then these common mistakes should be tolerated or acceptable [in the short-term], knowing that over time they can be corrected by the user, as language learning skills are developed. A sixty-percent correct usage tolerance in accepting a forty-percent error rate in a progressing new learner is acceptable.

Here are some examples of the most common misused words when writing and / or in speech [incorrect usage of accent, stress or pitch]:

Accept (v.): to receive willingly, to approve, to agree
Except (v., prep.): to exclude or to leave out

Ad (n.): an advertisement
Add (v.): to join, unite, combine or a mathematical sum

Affect (v.): to cause a change in something or someone
Effect (n.): a result

Ate (v.): past tense of eat
Eight (cardinal number): the number 8

Bass (n.): a voice, instrument, or sound of low pitch [bass drum]
Bass (n.): common European freshwater perch (fish)

Buy (v.): to purchase
By (prep., adv.): next to, beside, by way of something
Bye (n.): to express farewell (abbreviation for the word 'goodbye')

Cite (v.): to quote somebody as an example or as evidence
Sight (v., n.): to aim through a scope, the ability to see or be seen
Site (n.): the location of land or stored data (computer hard drive)

Desert (v.): to abandon
Dessert (n.): a sweet food

Dove (v.): past tense of dive
Dove (n.): a pigeon-like bird with a cooing voice [a white dove]

Elicit (v.): to draw out a response
Illicit (adj.): forbidden by law, rules or custom

For (prep.): in support, benefit, or in favor of
Fore (n., adj.): the front part, situated, placed or located in the front
Four (cardinal number): the number 4

Knew (v.): past tense of know
New (adj.): not existing before, recently produced or discovered

Know (v.): to be familiar with someone or something
No (n., det.): not any, negative reply of refusal

Object (v.): to express one's disapproval or disagreement
Object (n.): a thing that can be seen, touched or felt

Peace (n.): freedom from disturbance, war or violence; tranquil
Piece (n.): portion of an object or material by separating the whole

Principal (n., adj.): a person with the highest authority or position, first in order of importance
Principle (n.): a fundamental truth or belief

Raw (adj.): uncooked
Roar (v., n.): a loud deep sound, a loud deep sound made by an animal [especially a Lion]

Subject (v.): to cause or force to undergo a particular experience
Subject (n.): a person or thing being discussed or described

Their (det.): belonging to people or things previously mentioned
There (adv.): a place or position
They're (contraction): the contracted form for 'they are'

To (prep.): to express motion, or express attachment
Too (adv.): to a higher degree than is wanted or permissible; usually placed at the end of a clause and means also [e.g. I like it too].
Two (cardinal number): the number 2

Wander (v., n.): to walk around aimlessly, an act of wandering
Wonder (v., n.): a desire to know, a feeling of surprise

Weather (n.): atmospheric conditions
Whether (conj.): to express an opinion between two or more alternative possibilities

Ware (n.): a type of product as in 'stoneware or Wedgwood-ware'
Wear (v.): to have on one's body to clothe, decorate or protect
Where (adv.): in or to what place or location

Write (v.): to mark letters, words, or symbols on a surface
Right (adj.): morally good, justified, or acceptable

You're (contraction): the contracted form for 'you are'
Your (det.): belonging to that which the speaker is addressing

✣ Composition, Essay, or Article ✣

A *composition* is a collective body of sentences that has been organized into one or more paragraphs.

An *essay or article* is a short piece of nonfiction writing, which is usually written from an author's personal perspective. Essays are written for a number of purposes. A writer may want to:

1. analyze
2. propose
3. conclude
4. challenge
5. call readers to action
6. provide literary criticism
7. change attitudes
8. provoke thought
9. entertain
10. theorize
11. evaluate
12. recommend
13. express an observation
14. reflect
15. express feelings
16. request
17. give aesthetic pleasure
18. summarize
19. inform
20. persuade
21. publicly declare a political policy
22. provide instructions necessary to complete a task
23. argue for a particular point of view

Writers can be assigned to compose a short one paragraph composition, or with the use of transitional sentences can be coached toward writing more lengthy compositions, or a full essay of several hundred or thousand words, depending on their English language ability.

Transitional Sentence

A *transitional sentence* prepares and creates a smooth passage or evolution from one paragraph to the next. A successfully written transitional sentence will allow the reader to logically connect the topic and its supporting content of the previously read paragraph with the topic and supporting content of the upcoming paragraph.

This is an example of a transitional sentence that leads to the next topic:

> *Clearly, appropriate academic and emotional support are two key ingredients to improving the best possible chance for success in special needs students, as they pursue their studies and seek a happier life.* ***However, proactive positive parent evolvement is also essential and necessary.***

Revising and Editing

Drafting, revising and *editing* are the processes where a writer develops an overall holistic text, which is refined toward a finished work or final draft, to a specific word or page length. The processes of drafting and revising often overlap, as the writing process moves back and forth between the two stages.

Revision is an important stage in the writing process where the writer reviews the entire draft, and as needed, organizes, condenses, corrects sentences, paragraphs or sections and then adds additional information attempting to produce an accurate, consistent, and complete work. The writing process may involve many drafts requiring multiple revisions.

The editing process often begins with the author's preceding stages of drafting, revising and editing, continuing with collaboration between the author and / or authors and the editor and / or editors.

Editing involves reviewing text and identifying usage errors and ensuring style adherence. It also includes the correction of grammatical errors and inconsistencies in usages, misspellings, typographical errors (typos), the correction of punctuation and correcting errors in citations.

It is critical that a chosen editor is familiar with the subject being edited, or at least possess a passion for gaining additional personal knowledge for the topic. An editor must have refined essential skills, able to:

1. work to deadlines,
2. be reliable,
3. be accessible,
4. be ethical,
5. respect confidentiality,
6. pay attention to detail,
7. sustain prolonged focus while on task,
8. have good interpersonal skills; tact, and
9. most importantly, be compatible with the writer or writers.

⌘ Proofing ⌘

Proofreading is the final step before submitting work to an assessor, literary agent or publisher. The act of proofreading should be performed by the original writer, on the first and final occasion; however, writers usually have low energy levels and mental fatigue toward the end of the writing process, are often burdened with stress, and usually blind to their own errors. The inclusion of a qualified third-party (s) to proofread prior to the final review is essential (not the editor or editors of the project). This additional *'set-of-eyes'* should result in a higher quality of work.

⌘ Submitting or Publishing ⌘

Submitting

When *submitting* a composition of any kind, whether it be an assignment, report, journal or magazine article, or an essay, a writer should follow the strict guidelines outlined by the receiving organization. It is advised that a writer research these guidelines before the first word is written or typed into or onto any device.

Publishing

The question that a writer may be pondering is whether to self-publish or to submit their work directly to a literary agent or a publisher. Manuscripts that are submitted directly to a publisher are referred to as *unsolicited submissions*. These submissions are usually placed in a general pile, where the publisher's readers browse through them to identify the most appealing commercial manuscripts of sufficient quality with the greatest revenue potential, to be eventually referred to an acquisitions editor (s) for review.

Once the acquisitions editor (s) have narrowed down their choices from thousands of submissions, they send the manuscript to editorial staff. It's important to realize that unsolicited submissions have a very low rate of being accepted, with a very small percentage published; said to be about 2-5 percent of all annual manuscripts submitted to the publishing industry in the United States.

The alternative choice is to find a literary agent, or to self-publish. If self-publishing is of interest, a writer or author has access to a number of new technological publishing tools, resources, and services that are available from the self-publishing industry. Writers can self-publish their work as an e-book, where a manuscript is uploaded to a website from where it can be downloaded and read by anyone, or they can utilize the user-friendly, cost effective *'print-on-demand'* option.

Here are several print-on-demand online companies. This list has been provided with the intension of assisting with a starting point toward research and investigation.

Disclaimer: Use the following list at your own risk and / or discretion:

AA Printing	http://www.printshopcentral.com
Advantage Medina Group	http://www.amgbook.com
Angel Printing San Diego	http://www.angelprint.com
Apex Book Manufacturing	http://www.apexbm.com
Art Book Bindery	http://www.artbookbindery.com
Authorhouse	http://www.authorhouse.com
Aventine Press	http://www.aventinepress.com
Blitz Print Inc.	http://www.blitzprint.com
Blurb	http://www.blurb.com
Book Stand Publishing	http://www.ebookstand.com
Booklocker	http://www.booklocker.com
Createspace*	**http://www.createspace.com**
Dog Ear	http://www.eigology.com/dogear
Equilibrium	http://www.equilibriumbooks.com
Foremost Press	http://foremostpress.com
Infinity Publishing*	http://www.infinitypublishing.com
Inkwater Press	http://www.inkwaterpress.com
Instant (Fundcraft) Publishing	http://www.instantpublisher.com
iUniverse	http://www.iuniverse.com
Llumina	http://www.llumina.com
Lulu*	**http://www.lulu.com**
Outskirts Press	http://www.outskirtspress.com
Pleasant Word (WinePress)	http://www.pleasantword.com
Trafford	http://www.trafford.com
Virtual Bookworm	http://www.virtualbookworm.com
WingSpan*	http://www.wingspanpress.com
Wordclay*	http://www.wordclay.com
Xlibris*	http://www2.xlibris.com
Xulon Press	http://www.xulonpress.com

* Sites that I found inviting.

CHAPTER FOUR: CLASSROOM MANAGEMENT

WISDOM IS POWER

KEYS TO SUCCESS IN THE CLASSROOM

The most important action an effective teacher can accomplish is to create a positive, supportive, intellectual and emotional learning environment in the classroom, a system that encourages risks (Lowman, 1984), to explore and maximize opportunities toward personal and academic development.

Classroom management is simply allowing the facilitation of learning through the positive leadership of individuals as they engage toward planned objectives. A classroom management plan should also embrace structure and provide accountability for all participants.

A teacher should possess or acquire, through personal development, the skills necessary to successfully direct and manipulate an individual student, or a student group's positive energy, talents, and natural passion for learning, toward predetermined educational goals. A teacher should also anticipate, divert, convert and then channel disruptive energy, if possible at its infancy, so that maximum success in the classroom can occur for all those who are engaged.

Here are several suggestions toward the promotion of effective classroom management.

1. Classroom Expectations

   At the beginning of the school year, a teacher can work with students to develop a set of written classroom expectations (or rules), with an agreed reward and consequence system built in. This will provide the teacher with greater flexibility to monitor and manage the student group, absent of any bias.

This process allows accountability to the student-created system, making it more likely that the students will adhere to their own rules.

In a positive classroom environment students should be inspired to encourage each other. Within this environment peer pressure toward predetermined student-created expectations (rules) will naturally occur, leaving the teacher innocent if any action toward consequence is required.

If there is a mutual agreement to adopt a warning system into the student-created expectations (rules), to curve disruptive behavior, then the following suggestion called *'Soccer Rules'* may be useful; a positive variation of the 'three-strikes and your out' concept.

Soccer Rules Discipline:

> A small yellow laminated index-card, 3 X 5 inch (7.6 by 12 cm) is flashed toward the student who strayed from the established rule--as a passive warning. If a second warning is required, then with a little more urgency, flash a second yellow-card at the repeat offender. The class should self-manage as the offender's peers get involved and pressure the offender to curve their disruptive behavior. Receiving the final red-card, which results in the student's predetermined consequence being initiated, should be rare, keeping the threat of the final consequence being initiated a real possibility.

2. Be 'Fair' but 'Firm'

   Objectivity and patience is paramount, as is clear boundaries for everyone involved; students, coworkers, and school administration, built on solid high professional and personal ethics. A teacher's personal boundaries need to be aligned with consistency.

3. Use Seating Plans

   Different activities will require movement in the classroom of both students and furniture. To achieve a positive learning environment, conducive to reaching the fullest potential of all students, consideration should be given to what works best for each activity, the individual, and what seating arrangements will assist with positive delivery, as well as assisting with implementing the classroom management strategy. There are advantages and disadvantages to either fixed or flexible seating plans, which a teacher will experience and then adjust to accordingly. Time is an ally, so experimenting and then learning from the results is time well spent. Wisdom grows as mistakes are made, and mistakes made are only another way of doing something before making an adjustment.

Students do not often adjust well to change, so minimize it where possible. Two to four different seating plans can be created according to the various activity types that may be planed, such as: lectures, presentations, group-work according to varying group size (four, six, or eight students etc.), study-group seating plans according to each individual's learning style and compatibility, and so on.

It is best practice to take attendance absent of any disruption to any activity's flow. Take attendance according to seating plans and empty seats.

4. Apply Active Learning in the Classroom

    Research by Chickering and Gamson (1987), suggest that students must do more than just listen, as in traditional unchanged *'row and line'* delivered lectures. Students must be actively engaged and involved in instructional activities that involves *'doing'* and *'thinking'* about what they are doing [finding solutions as they process relative information]. Some cognitive research has shown that a significant number of students have learning styles that are best served by pedagogical techniques other than lecturing (Bonwell, 1991).

    Keeping students awake, focused, and aware of a teacher's presence, and to the possibility that the teacher may call on them at any given time to express an answer to a question, or give an opinion, is an ongoing process, which accommodates a pedagogical active-learning strategy.

    Here are some tips a teacher may choose to implement:

    - To pause several times during a presentation, for two minutes for each occasion, will allow thoughts to be consolidated and notes to be updated. By doing this, students will learn and retain significantly more information (Ruhl, Hughes, and Schloss, 1987).

    - To model content with brief demonstrations, repeated occasionally to reinforce new ideas and language.

    - To occasionally use ungraded assessment activities or short quizzes followed by a class discussion of the group's outcome. This discussion will promote long-term retention of the presented information and will provide motivation toward further learning and involvement (McKeachie et al., 1986).

- To use red or green paddles that are raised to reflect a yes / no answer to questions, or issue sets of cards numbered from one to ten to a panel of responsible student judges, to grade peers' answers, [or the teacher's]; at the conclusion of each participant's short-presentation.

5. Student Discipline

If corrective action is required, then discipline should always be conducted quietly and privately. Screaming at a student from across the classroom may shame the student in front of their peers, resulting in the erosion of mutual respect and overall rapport.

6. Being Punctual

A teacher should always start classes on time! This example sends a clear message that being present is important. If a student challenges their responsibility of being punctual, then action should be taken quickly, sending a firm message that the value of punctuality is non-negotiable.

A teacher should also end classes on time. Inconsistency may result in a student feeling anxious or uneasy. Once students are allowed to leave the classroom early, they will begin routinely winding down, packing up their backpacks, and chatting prematurely; furthermore, if the teacher regularly goes over the scheduled time, they risk the loss of rapport [any teacher-student harmony that has been built up over time].

7. Proactive Monitoring of the Classroom

A teacher who actively monitors and moves around the classroom, maintaining a proactive presence with brief eye-contact, will convey a message that individual attention and personal care is present. In addition, each student should be held accountable for retaining or recording the information presented at that moment.

Actively monitoring the classroom also prevents small disturbances from escalating into bigger ones, and also heightens students' awareness toward the belief that their teacher is watching them, ready to support them when needed.

8. Tone of Voice; Keeping it vocal with purpose

Tone of voice, which reflects mood and authenticity, is an effective tool if used positively; essential in settling down students and focusing their attention toward tasks. Speaking in monotone and lacking enthusiasm will put students to sleep or cause them to seek alternative activities to occupy their time, often leading to distractions. A teacher can vocalize helpful reminders as needed, and offer a choice if students seem stuck or uninterested. A teacher must provide positive feedback and encouragement, ask directed questions, and use appropriate humor to change mood.

When a teacher addresses their students, they need to talk slowly, but naturally; being nervous usually causes a person to rush through information. Clear pronounced language not only assists with acquiring the new language, but it also reinforces the importance of what is being said and also communicates confidence.

Frequent pauses are a technique that can cause students who are not tuned in to retune their attention toward what the teacher is saying and doing, looking up from a zombie-like state, re-establishing eye contact, and drawing students in.

Each class may differ from the next and each day differs from another. If one technique doesn't work, try another until eventually all the experience gained will naturally influence reactionary habits.

9. Maintain Strict Course Assessment Grading Policies

Students expect and work best with consistently enforced policies, rules and procedures. Straying from the above, such as an established 'grading model', may cause a student to challenge the teacher's decisions and / or may result in being seen as a pushover.

10. Inappropriate Behavior

A teacher needs to be fully conscious of signs of any racism, sexual harassment, or bullying toward any member of the class. It must be clear, through example, that belittling others in any way, shape, or form, or derogatory comments about any person, race, religious group, for whatever reason (s), will simply not be acceptable or tolerated.

11. Students with Special Needs

Students identified with possible special needs must be referred to the appropriate school staff. In most cases it is not a teacher's responsibility to professionally access a student's special needs, but it is the teacher's responsibility to support students with them. The teacher can be sympathetic and supportive, but taking on the role as a student's counselor can cause potential problems.

12. Limitations and Boundaries

    A teacher should feel secure with who they are, know their limitations, and adhere to personal boundaries, and most of all, know when to ask for help.

Potential Problems that May Occur

Monitoring the classroom is a huge part of classroom management. Two things to be aware of are what students 'do' while they believe their teacher is watching them and what students 'do' when they believe their teacher's attention is focused elsewhere. Students want to impress their peers, but also their teacher, the assessor. Attitude and work rates may reflect this. A teacher should have a plan as to how to assess an individual's involvement and progress from a distance, intervening only as needed.

It is often thought that a teacher has eyes in the back of their head, but the fact is they don't. A teacher should be careful not to consistently have their back to their students, to face as many students as possible, so that full monitoring of the environment can occur. A teacher should not get too involved with an individual group, so that ignoring the needs of others is kept to a minimum.

Methods that Encourage Engagement

Many successful teachers deploy an effective method of delivery with humor and or being entertaining. Their bubbly, energetic personalities, or charisma, attract interest and assist with student engagement. This method is particularly effective during the introduction and modeling stages and the delivery of the core lesson, before any reinforcement through individual or group practice.

It is important to note that a teacher should be extremely careful not to lose a student (s) in the entertainment; striking a balance between being an entertainer verses being an effective facilitator of the learning required in progress toward educational objectives. The use of prolonged humor, and being entertaining, should not distract from, or become an obstacle or barrier to educational goals and objectives. Eventually the facilitator needs to step back and allow learning to occur through the students' 'doing,' if language acquisition is to occur.

Cross-cultural Awareness and Sensitivity

Cross-cultural awareness and *cross-cultural sensitivity* are important factors to implementing successful classroom management techniques because they deal with interpersonal communication.

Cross-cultural awareness and cross-cultural sensitivity is not the same thing. Being culturally sensitive implies a willingness to observe and attempt to understand other individuals and / or cultural groups' traditions, and ways of life. Culturally sensitive people attempt to free themselves from preconceptions about another's culture, free of prejudice, or centric stereotyping.

Cross-cultural awareness occurs when a person obtains cultural knowledge of another ethnic group. Usually there must be internal adjustments made to a person's thinking, in terms of their attitude and values. The learning process will require the qualities of open mindedness and flexibility.

Once an open-minded person has allowed change to occur, and they have increased their cultural knowledge, they can then become sensitive to the differences of another individual or group. The changes made will potentially affect relationships and the way a person communicates with a person or group of people of another culture.

William Howell (1997) writes of the *Four Levels of Cultural Awareness*:

Unconscious Incompetence

This has also been called the state of *'blissful ignorance.'* At this stage, a person is unaware of cultural differences. It does not occur to them that they may be making cultural mistakes or that they may be misinterpreting much of the behavior going on around them. They have no reason not to trust their instincts.

Conscious Incompetence

A person now realizes that differences exist between the way they and the local people behave, though they understand very little about what these differences are, how numerous they might be, or how deep they might go. They know there's a problem here, but they're not sure about the size of it. They're not so sure of their instincts anymore, and they realize that there are some things they don't understand. They may start to worry about how hard it's going to be to figure these people out.

Conscious Competence

They know cultural differences exist, they know what some of these differences are, and they try to adjust their own behavior accordingly. It doesn't come naturally yet—they have to make a conscious effort to behave in culturally appropriate ways— but they are much more aware of how their behavior is coming across to the local people. They are in the process of replacing old instincts with new ones. They know now they might be able to figure these people out if they can remain objective.

Unconscious Competence

They no longer have to think about what they're doing in order to do the right thing. Culturally appropriate behavior is now second nature to them; trusting their instincts because they have been reconditioned by the new culture. It takes little effort now for them to be culturally sensitive.

QUOTE:

"If man is to survive, he will have learned to take a delight in the essential differences between men [and women] and between cultures. He [or she] will learn that differences in ideas and attitudes are a delight, part of life's exciting variety, not something to fear."

Gene Roddenberry

CHAPTER FIVE:
TEACHING PERSPECTIVES

APPROACHES and METHODS

English Language Curriculum Delivery

There are many methods of teaching the English language, which can be categorized into three main approaches. These approaches are the *structural*, *functional* and the *interactive*.

✤ Structural Approaches ✤

The *structural approach* views language as a system of structurally related elements to code meaning, such as the use of grammar. There are two main methods within the structural approach. These methods are the *grammar translation* and the *audio-lingual method*.

Grammar-translation Method

The *grammar translation method* typically places an ESL teacher at the front of a classroom with seating arranged in straight rows and lines, where the teacher provides instruction on vocabulary, usually accompanied by a direct translation, as well as providing explanations on grammar rules and use. This vocabulary, and the grammar rules, are exposed with the intention of student memorization.

This method has been scrutinized with a predominate agreement among seasoned English language teaching professionals that the method, by itself, is ineffective. Nevertheless, the grammar-translation method remains the most commonly practiced method of English teaching in most developing countries, and in some conservative developed countries.

Audio-lingual Method

The *audio-lingual method* is based on the behaviorist theory where the belief is that students be trained through a system of reinforcement techniques, such as language drills (also known as *pattern practice*) to reinforce the new language learned (Richards, 1986). These drills include, but are not limited to:

Repetition:

This type of drill is a method of familiarizing students with a specific structure or formulaic expression (Doff, 1990). This is achieved by having the students, or student group (simultaneously) repeat an utterance when they hear it from their teacher.

Here is a repetition-drill, when introducing the prepositions *'on'* and *'under'* to a student group:

Teacher: There's a book *on* the table.
Student: There's a book *on* the table.
Teacher: There's a pencil *on* the book.
Student: There's a pencil *on* the book.
Teacher: There's a book *under* the pencil.
Student: There's a book *under* the pencil.

Replacement or Substitution:

This type of drill is used to expand a previously learnt core-dialog by replacing a variable within a sentence. The core-dialog can be written on the blackboard or projected on the projector-screen, with the word to be replaced underlined. A list of practice variables can be written on the blackboard next to the core-dialog, as an example.

A variable replacement is practiced, with the teacher eventually coaching toward the creation of an additional substitute (s), impromptu variable (s).

Here is an example of a student-group phrase-replacement substitution-drill:

Teacher: What do you want to do on the weekend.
Student 1: I want to go to a movie.
Teacher: What do you want to do on the weekend?
Student 2: I want to go shopping at the mall.
Teacher: What do you want to do on the weekend?
Student 3: I want to stay home and sleep.

Here is an example of a student-group substitution-drill using two simple teacher-cued words as a *prompt:*

Prompt: *country and activity*
Teacher: I want to travel to <u>New Zealand</u>.
I'd like to <u>visit Te Papa Museum</u>.
Student 1: I want to travel to <u>France</u>.
I'd like to <u>visit the Eiffel Tower</u>.
Student 2: I want to travel to <u>England</u>.
I'd like to <u>visit Buckingham Palace</u>.

Experimentally advanced students should be encouraged to test unfamiliar language after the core-dialog's structure has been learnt, such as this potential response:

Prompt: *country and activity*
Student: I want to travel to <u>a historical place in Japan</u>.
I'd like to <u>visit Nara where my friend lives</u>.

Transformation:

This type of drill is used to rephrase a teacher's utterance (change the structure of the sentence), with the use of cues. Additionally, a student would be directed to replace the variables. Here are some examples:

Positive to negative:

Prompt: *subject in school*
Teacher: I **like** to study <u>Math</u> at school.
Student: I **don't like** to study <u>Art</u> at school.

Statement to question:

Prompt: *favourite food*
Teacher: I **like** to eat <u>udong noodles</u>.
Student: **Do you like** to eat <u>Rice cakes</u>?

One tense to another:

Prompt: *moments of time (when?)*
Teacher: I'**ll go** to the movies <u>on the weekend</u>.
Student: <u>Last week</u> I **went** to the movies.

Active to passive voice:

Prompt: *a gift*
Teacher: I **gave** my mother <u>a new purse</u>.
Student: I **was given** <u>a movie ticket</u> by my mother.

Singular to plural subject:

Prompt: *transportation to school*

Teacher: The **student** rides the bus to school everyday.

Student: The **students** take their bikes to school everyday.

If a student was to produce correct English vocabulary and usage, this would incite a teacher to award positive feedback while incorrect vocabulary and usage would result in negative feedback.

In the audio-lingual method, students are taught the English language directly, absent of any native language support to explain new words or grammar. The teacher presents a model of a sentence and then the students repeat it. This technique would then be expanded, replacing specific variables within the same sentence structure. The students would practice the particular construct, and its variables, trying to memorize them until they are able to spontaneously use it appropriately. In this model students don't have the freedom to create their own output; the teacher controls this. This differs from communicative language learning.

Functional Approach

The *functional approach* views language as a catalyst to accomplish a certain function, such as asking or giving directions. There is one main method to a functional approach. This method is known as the *oral approach.*

Situational Language Teaching

Situational language teaching is considered by applied linguistics as an oral approach to acquiring a second language, by learning vocabulary and then practicing and developing reading skills. This method focuses on behavioral psychology; the processes of learning the language, not the conditions of learning. These processes are:

1. A student receives language instruction, both orally and in written form.
2. The information is then practiced by the student with a strong emphasis on the oral form (usually with the participation in a variety of drills), and with less emphasis practiced in the written form.
3. The information is memorized to the point of it becoming knowledge, where it can be spontaneously recited as a habit.

✄ Interactive Approaches ✄

The *interactive approach* views language as a catalyst for the creation and maintenance of interpersonal relationships. There are several methods within the interactive approach. These are, but not limited to:

Direct or Natural Method

The *direct method* of teaching the English language, also referred to as the *natural method,* is arguably the most recent and the most promising approach to language teaching and acquisition. In this method, a teacher will avoid the use of the learners' first or native language, exposing students to only the new target or second language.

Dr. Stephen Krashen, a *'professor emeritus'* at the University of Southern California, USA, who has published more than 350 papers and books, contributing to the fields of bilingual education and second language acquisition, theorizes that *'communication'* is the main function of language and that the main focus for English language teachers (ELTs) is to teach communicative skills. He views language as a vehicle for *'communicating meanings'* and *'messages'.* According to Krashen, *'acquisition'* can only take place when a student comprehends messages in the *target language* (TL). Here is a simple model of the processes associated with teaching a *'direct'* or *'natural language'* method:

Step One: The observation stage

> Students listen to teacher-talk as they observe classroom real-life objects, content within visual materials, or basic pantomimes. Natural, age and English-level specific target language is set to a specific context, accompanied by gestures to decipher (un-code) and then reinforce the target language being presented.

Step Two: The initial interpersonal language stage

> Students are asked simple yes / no questions that, at first, only require a one-word utterance. More complex **wh~** questions and answers, involving more advanced processing, can follow, slowly developing the students knowledge toward greater interpersonal interaction. These **wh~** questions might reflect one of the following:

> > What... Asking for information about something, a reason, or determining why,

> > When... Asking about moments of time,

Where...   Asking in what place, at what place, or in what position,

Which...   Asking a choice,

Who...   Asking what or which person,

Whose...   Asking about ownership,

Why...   Asking for what reason or purpose.

Step Three: The acquisition stage

After establishing the core-dialog through observation and interpersonal interaction, the teacher can move onto the acquisition stage. Active-learning techniques are essential for increased development, such as group-work or whole-class activities. These types of active-learning activities reinforce or further develop the target language within the learner.

At this stage, other borrowed methods can be adapted and introduced, such as the *Total Physical Response Method* developed by Dr. James J. Asher, *'professor-emeritus'* of psychology, at San Jose State University, in the USA. Asher claims that language is internalized by learners of a second language, through a process of code-breaking. This process allows for extended listening periods where a student develops comprehension before they attempt personal production of the target language.

In the direct or natural method of teaching, the model is teacher-centered or teacher-focused. The onus is squarely placed on the teacher, who must maintain the students' attention on core lexical words or vocabulary, create the correct atmosphere and classroom environment that is conducive to the students reaching their highest potential, and select the appropriate materials and activities, so that the students have the potential to acquire the target language successfully.

In this model, students are seen as a processor of information. The teacher presents information that is slightly beyond the students' current competence. A sixty-percent student-retention and recall of information, at any given point, is considered successful. The teacher can build from this success, keeping in mind that students are not all alike. Each student's ability will vary according to their level of linguistic development.

Communicative Language Teaching (CLT)

Communicative language teaching, also known as *the communicative approach to the teaching of the English language* (simply, *'the communicative approach'*), is an approach to the Teaching of English to Speakers of Other Languages (TESOL) or the Teaching of English as a Foreign Language (TEFL) that emphasizes interaction as both the main focus and the ultimate learning objective.

Communicative language teaching can involve the following activities:

1. board or card-game creation, or the playing commercial games,

2. English based skits, pantomimes, or role plays,

3. English language focused teacher designed games,

4. interactive teacher and student presentations,

5. one-on-one, small group, or whole-class discussions, in English (choose age specific, culturally sensitive material to discuss),

6. pair or group-work conducted in English,

7. cooperative student group surveys, or

8. teacher and student interviews on age specific subject matter.

Task-based Language Teaching (TBLT)

The *task-based language teaching model*, also known as *task-based instruction* (TBI), is a refined communicative language teaching method. The philosophy behind this method is to introduce a student to genuine language, followed by an assignment, so that the student can conduct meaningful follow-up tasks using the target language; a student-centered method. These tasks can include:

- buying something at the store,
- interviewing a member of the community, or
- giving directions to a fellow student as they walk to the bank.

Success can be assessed by monitoring a student or student group's correctly completed outcomes and a written assignment composed based on their experience. This model is relevant only if tasks are specifically designed with real life situations appropriate to that student or student group.

Here is a simple six-step model of the processes associated with using the task-based method:

Step One: The preparation

The teacher outlines all of the lesson requirements and expectations. The task's necessary core-dialog, and its constructs, are introduced and / or modeled by presenting directive images, or a video demonstrating the task.

The outline is presented as 'suggestions only,' encouraging the use of creativity to accomplish goals, learning naturally through the potential correction by others in the community or from adjustment through personal experience.

Step Two: Practice

The practice stage is where students reinforce the information given to them in oral, written, and through dramatization, preparing them before they perform the task in a real-life environment.

The hope is that dialog can be memorized to the point of it becoming knowledge, where it can be spontaneously recited when needed.

Step Three: The active learning task

A student performs the task; however, small groups are better suited for this activity; students can give support to each other through peer-teaching. A best-practice scenario suggests that a teacher should be an observer, not a participant.

Step Four: Reflection and report creation

Students are given time to reflect on the task processes, construct and organize notes, and then create a composition to an assigned word length to present to the class. The teacher monitors progress and assists with grammatical questions.

Step Five: Presentation

One-by-one students present their work to the class. Students are encouraged to interact with the presenter providing questions and feedback.

Step Six: Teacher analysis

>The teacher reflects on the overall process. The following questions should be considered:
>
>1. Were the objectives met?
>2. Were there any language constructs that need to be covered or were there any forms that were not used that need to be addressed in future classes.
>3. Can the process be improved?

Language Immersion Method

Language immersion delivers academic content through the medium of a foreign or target language (L2), providing support to speakers of other languages as well as first language (L1) maintenance.

There are three immersion categories. These are:

1. Foreign Language Immersion

   Foreign language immersion programs are designed for students who speak the native home language (L1). Students receive instruction through the medium of a second language (L2), such as: Spanish, Chinese, Japanese, Korean, Maori, etc.

2. Dual Immersion

   Dual immersion programs are designed for students who speak the native home language (L1), as well as for students whose native language is the target or immersion language (L2). The objective is to develop strong bilingualism. In this model, content is delivered through the medium of the immersion language for part of the day, and through the second language the second part of the day.

3. Indigenous Immersion

   Indigenous immersion programs are designed for indigenous communities desiring to maintain the use of the native language by delivering elementary school content through the medium of that language. Two examples of successful immersion programs are:

   1. Ka Papahana Kaiapuni Hawai'i (USA), the Hawaiian immersion program.
   2. Kura Kaupapa Māori, the Aotearoa (New Zealand) Māori language immersion program. The philosophy

and practice is to reflect Māori cultural values with the aim of revitalizing Māori language, knowledge (Kaupapa) and culture. This approach has been successful in many Māori language preschools (Kohanga Reo) throughout Aotearoa, New Zealand.

Language Submersion

The difference between *language immersion* and *language submersion* is that an immersion class is where a student learns a second language (L2) at the same level and time as their classmates; while in the latter (submersion), one or two students will learn the foreign language (L2), which is the first language (L1) for the rest of the class, thus they either *'sink-or-swim'* instead of being gradually immersed in the new language.

Dogme Language Teaching

Dogme language teaching, also known as *Dogme ELT*, is a communicative approach to the teaching of the English language, driven by Scott Thornbury an Associate Professor of English Language Studies at the New School, in New York, USA.

Dogme ELT has a number of main principles (Thornbury, 2005). In summary, these principles are:

1. Interactivity

   The most direct route to learning is found in the interactivity between teachers and students and amongst the students themselves.

2. Engagement

   Students are most engaged by content they provide or have created themselves.

3. The Social and Dialogic Processes

   Learning is social and dialogic, where knowledge is co-constructed rather than 'transmitted' or 'imported' from teacher to learner.

4. Scaffolding

   Language can be mediated through conversation, especially when supported and developed by the teacher.

5. Emergence

   Language and grammar emerge organically, under the right conditions, rather than being acquired.

6. Affordances

   One of a teacher's primary roles in the classroom is to optimize language-learning affordances. For example, directing attention features of the emergent language.

7. Freedom of Voice

   The student's 'voice' is respectfully recognized, accepting their beliefs, knowledge, experiences, concerns and desires as valid content in the language learning classroom environment.

8. Empowerment

   Freeing the classroom from third-party, imported materials empowers both teachers and learners.

9. Relevance

   Texts, when used, should have relevance for the learner.

10. Ideological Baggage

    Teachers and learners should reevaluate their view of EFL materials—to become critical users of such texts.

QUOTE:

"The important thing is not so much that every child should be taught, as that every child should be inspired to obtain the self-motivation to learn."

John Lubbock

CHAPTER SIX:
LESSON PRESENTATION

THE FUNDAMENTALS

✖ Physical Learning Environment ✖

The *physical learning environment* contributes significantly toward effective teaching and improvements in a student's learning and achievement. Research into student achievement strongly supports the notion that a physical environment must entice and inspire students toward self-motivation and a desire to be present in the classroom, similar to the ways cafe's and shopping malls influence and invite foot-traffic with gimmicks and desirable ergonomic design, rather than the traditional four-walls-and-a-blackboard space of a traditional classroom being purely an administrative functional space (Bunting, 2004).

There is a full range of research that reports on optimal teaching and learning space, with a predominant shift toward an open-plan holistic classroom model. In this model students are able to learn in ways suited to their own individual learning style with strategic seating plans and classroom design more likely to accommodate different teaching and learning contexts.

Schools are a place where students inhabit. As they participate in various classes, extracurricular activities, and socialize, they interconnect and develop lasting relationships with peers and teachers. ESL teachers become mentors and representatives of Western culture. A teacher's passion, rhetoric, and actions will influence observant young minds. A physical classroom environment is an extension of this influence, where a student's cognitive and behavioral development may also be effected, creating and contributing to their overall perspective from which they see and interpret the world.

Seating Plans

On the first day of classes, students can be a little anxious about a new student-teacher relationship, moreover they can also be uncertain with the new physical environment and the potential classroom dynamic. Consider straight rows and lines as an initial arrangement to send a message to students that there is an authority in that classroom, a pack-leader. Young-learners and teenagers in particular require structure, boundaries, and mutual respect, if order and cohesion are to be established. Rapport can be built and maintained after this establishment.

A big part of establishing a teacher's authority in the classroom is to control the students' environment, not vice-versa. Leaving the desks in straight rows and lines should only occur if it supports the learning objective. The teacher may return to a straight *'rows and lines'* model as a way of reinforcing order. However, if a horseshoe or any other seating plan is the classroom standard to promote control and coherence, then that model would become the standard to fall back on.

Here are some possible classroom seating arrangements common in the ESL classroom:

Rows and Lines:

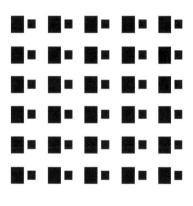

Place a student or students who challenge classroom rules as far from their accomplices as possible; moreover, assigning specific seats to a specific individual is a great way to take attendance.

This seating plan works well for testing, individual study or project work.

Horseshoe:

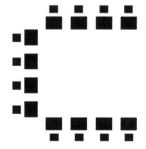

This arrangement is perhaps the most versatile, where a teacher can maintain eye contact with all students, almost simultaneously.

It also provides space for modeling, group-work on the floor, double-lines, skits, and other reinforcement activities.

Circle:

This is a variation of the horseshoe arrangement.

Form a single circle of the entire class group, or form several small circles of five to ten students at various places around the ESL classroom (similar to clusters).

Access to any student by the teacher will allow monitoring, support, and disciplinary intervention when needed.

Clusters:

Several groups of four to five students form social pods where peer teaching occurs.

As in the circle arrangement, clusters also allow access to any student by the teacher, and will allow monitoring, support, and intervention when needed.

Pairs:

This is a variation of the cluster arrangement; a mini cluster.

Two students form a less threatening pairing where they can work together for study, projects and small independent activities. This seating arrangement is perfect for paired study, using flashcards.

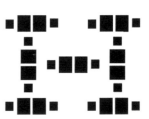

The most important consideration for any seating configuration is that a student must always have an unobstructed view of all instruction. Before class begins, a teacher should test the seating by sitting in various seats around the room to see if the student will be able to see the position from where the teacher lectures, shows a video, models dialog, acts out a role play, displays the digital projector, or writes on the black or whiteboard.

Digital Technology in the ESL Classroom

The Twenty-first Century's acceleration in technology and our youth's passion, admiration of and fixation on it, is transforming the way people conduct day-to-day activities, how they globally socialize, and how they lead and manage domestic and international business. There is the existence of digital dependency in developed countries, which is growing at a tremendous rate in developing countries. This growth initially takes hold in the urban areas and then naturally spreads outward, to the rural areas. It is inevitable that this technological dependency will influence a change in the current education delivery paradigm and in culture itself. Students are adapting! 'Old-school' educators will need to adapt or gamble with isolation.

Educators who are interacting with the high-tech youth of tomorrow have a responsibility to keep pace, or risk the disengagement of their students. If teachers are to engage and motivate students, they must incorporate familiar electronic gadgets and applications into the classroom setting. A majority of students are preprogrammed to accept the technology change in their classroom, or school environment, as similar technology is increasingly prevalent in their lives outside the classroom.

> **Factoid:** Fifty-five million homes in the USA have at least one iPhone, iPad, iPod or Mac computer. Of those homes, the average ownership of an apple product is three. One-in-10 homes that aren't currently in that group of ownership plan to join the group next year. Overall, the United States average household has 1.6 Apple devices, with almost one-quarter planning to buy at least one more in the next year (Gralnick, 2012).

The technology is also superbly adapted to compliment a commonly held belief among educational psychologists and experienced English language teachers, that is, that students have a variety of learning preferences and styles. This technology provides a combination of stimulus, such as: sound and music, color, graphics, animation, video, and an opportunity for students to engage and participate in active learning through interactive software.

Start with a Single Step

Most classrooms around the world are at best four walls, a few desks and chairs, and if a teacher is really fortunate a blackboard or whiteboard is available. The teacher and the textbook are the tools of the trade; the teacher speaks, students listen, and students are then assessed.

It is accepted practice in South Korea to have ESL middle and high-school classrooms with at least one or several electronic tools at an

English language teacher's disposal, such as:

- an interactive whiteboard or smart-board,
- overhead digital projectors,
- Blue-screen technology (used to create the illusion of a background that isn't really there, projecting the combined image of the teacher and the digitally created image on a big-screen that students see, as the teacher models dialog on a purpose built stage at the front of the classroom),
- touch-screen workstation pods, using the latest educational interactive software, placed around the school in hallways,
- purpose build cubicles with real life "sets" where students enact or reenact real-life situations (role play scenes, such as: ordering at the cafe, buying a ticket at a train-station, or meeting someone at the airport, etc.),
- hardwired and wireless high-speed internet on up-to-date computers with large flat-screens.

On the other hand, in many developing countries, such as Thailand, Vietnam, parts of China and the Middle East, and surprisingly also in a technologically advanced country like Japan, it is common to experience isolated schools in rural areas, where four walls, a few desks and chairs, and a rather big blackboard at one end of the classroom, being the only tools an English language teacher will have access to.

It doesn't matter if an English language teacher is new or experienced—both bring vast experience to the job, in one form or another. It is important that a teacher keeps in mind that the working environment cannot change from 'what a teacher knows', but can only change from 'what a teacher does' with 'what they know'. The injection of even a modest level of technology in some isolated organizations can represent an enormous expansion to current beliefs and may challenge routines and habits. However, as the Chinese philosopher Laozi, a record-keeper at the Zhou Dynasty Court wrote, "The journey of a thousand miles begins beneath one's feet," or most commonly translated by English speakers as, "A journey of a thousand miles begins with a single step."

Here is a personal experience. When I faced this dilemma at a private high school in North-central Japan, the first step I had to consider was to ask a simple question in order to seek support. However, it can be a challenge for some inexperienced teachers to ask for support. This can be a hurdle, an obstacle, or a barrier to progress or to potential success. Progress can be protracted or can be eroded if a teacher is afraid to ask. Asking is one of the most powerful and neglected tools a successful teacher has. A teacher should resist creating fear of rejection, or the potential anxiety that hearing the word 'no' may bring. If the answer is 'no', they are no worse off than when they started. If they do receive the answer they are seeking, then they are progressing as hoped.

Before asking any question within an organization, a teacher should carefully consider whom the right person is to approach. In my case, it was a young Information Technology teacher. My question to him was, is there a digital projector and a portable projector-screen available for my use. I tactfully explained, clearly and specifically, what I hoped to achieve. I stated that I respected his knowledge of technology and would appreciate his guidance as I walked into the unknown.

His first response wasn't the supportive solution I was hopeful for. He politely said, "Why?" I realized that I needed to step back quickly and try to understand the root to his response, that decades of blackboard 'n' chalk delivery had been the acceptable medium for non-technical subjects, to this point, and was the norm. The concept of using technology as an ELT tool for delivering curriculum was not easily understood. Such IT equipment is stereotypically seen as only necessary in an IT specific classroom, or provided in a special projector classroom or lecture room, where all teachers have access on a reservation basis.

There seemed to be a little apprehension or cautious resistance to my request at first, after-all it would mean expanding or changing the current paradigm. It seemed as if the question he needed to process was to why any English language teacher would require anything but their voice and a blackboard to deliver an oral communication class. To be brief, after three months of passive, but polite nudging, one morning I found a digital projector placed on my desk and a note directing me to the location of a portable projector-screen. This was the tipping point toward the gradual injection of technology into my ESL classroom.

Over the next three months, I prepared all my lessons using either PowerPoint or Keynote. Flashcards, games, dialog, and images to support setting context were all visually projected on the screen at the front of the class. Portable laptop speakers provided enough sound to get me by. Slowly the Head-teacher, Vice-principal and the school's Director casually wondered past my classroom, sneaking a peek with curiosity. I quickly created an English game based on an old American television game show, called 'The Family Feud'. I tested the game-show presentation on my students, who absolutely loved it.

Senior school staff continued to observe me until one day I invited those key staff to enter my class, asking them to provide feedback on my teaching at its completion. They agreed and attended. On the day of the presentation, I set up 'Very Important Person's' (VIP) desks, at the back of the room. Once the VIPs were seated, I distributed worksheets to all students, also providing a set of the VIP group. I started the presentation resulting in all students and VIPs being deeply involved, with intensity and excitement. At the conclusion of the session, I received a thumbs-up by all VIP attendees. The seed was now planted. Key decision makers observed the successful use of technology in the ESL classroom resulting in acceptance.

Over time, the stream of curious colleagues increased. Using technology in the classroom by many subject teachers is now a common topic in the teacher's room with many teachers adopting the practice.

Lesson Planning

Foundation

A lesson plan is a detailed descriptive summary of a teacher's single lesson. Its purpose is to assist and guide the teacher in their instruction and facilitation of learning the English language. A lesson plan may be governed by requirements mandated by governing organizations, the school, or the private company for which the teacher is employed.

There are several considerations that should go into lesson planning. These are, but not limited to:

Create a profile of the target-individual or group:

It is important to have a clear understanding of *who* will be taught. A teacher may want to find the answers to these questions:

- Is the class a private one-on-one lesson or a group of students?
- If it is a group of students, what is the group size, gender, or intellectual level or their social maturity?
- What is the individual or group's English language ability in the various English language skill areas of reading, writing, speaking, or listening?
- Are the students of the same group at multiple levels?
- What are the expectations of the group or the organization for which the teacher is employed?
- Does the culture or religious backgrounds of the student or student group require special attention, action, or sensitivity?
- To what degree has there been any previous English language exposure?

Gain knowledge and an understanding of the teaching environment and any requirements:

Each organization will differ with the requirements they mandate. Lesson plan tasks will need to be written so that systematic progress toward predetermined objectives will meet or exceed the expectations of the organization.

To further empower a teacher before planning their annual lessons, they may want to find the answers to these questions:

- Are there any achievement requirements?
- What is the length and frequency of each class?
- Is there a set curriculum, or is the teacher required and expected to create their own lessons, with or without any guidance?
- Are there any internal or external assessment requirements that need to be meet?
- What are the administrative requirements for the course (attendance, report cards, teacher / parent interviews, reporting, etc.)?
- Are there any relative short, medium, or long-term goals / objectives to be aware of in the organization's strategic plan?

Another important thing to consider is the psychological factors associated with the stakeholders: the student or student group, organization, or greater community.

Students have been enrolled into a school or academy for differing reasons. Sometimes law, such as mandatory attendance at an elementary, middle, or high school, mandates this enrollment. Other times parent-influence is present with forced enrollment into an English language school, which meets the parent's wishes, but not the student's; or it may simply be that the student chooses to attend. No matter what the motivating factors may be, questions still need to be considered, such as:

- Why are the students attending the school, or more specifically, why are they attending the English language class? Is their presence by choice (an elective) or forced (a mandatory subject, or is attendance demanded from parents)?
- What are the determining factors for having an English language course provided at the school? Is it mandated by the government, community driven, or does the student population seek it?

- What can stakeholders get from the presence of this course? Is the acquiring of the English language useful to the learner to enter higher education or to gain suitable employment in the future?

A little research into the above factors will empower any teacher toward becoming an effective English language teacher. If a teacher can determine the psychological factors that drive the need for their presence at the organization, then meeting the objectives and expectations of those who govern them will become a little less of a challenge.

Lesson Timing

Lesson types vary, as do each organization's class duration. English language acquisition activities have no specific order per-say; rather, the module order is often influenced by various factors, such as:

A Student's Age

Often activities that are focused toward young-learners require shorter periods of delivery time with frequent change. They should compliment a young mind's short attention span and should be age-appropriate.

Increased repetition is necessary for young-learners, welcomed and acceptable; whereas, the technique of the over-use of repetition for advanced or older adult students more likely to be irritating.

To reinforce this point, reflect back to your own observation of a younger sibling or another's child who watches the same cartoon or movie repeatedly, never seeming to get bored? It drives adults bonkers. As adults, we usually are limited to the initial viewing, and if a movie is exceptional, we may watch it a second or third time.

The Student's Previous Exposure to the English Language and Their Current Target Language Level

Lower-level students, such as false-beginners, beginners, elementary, and lower-intermediates, will require more introduction work (modeling) and controlled practice.

Higher-level students, such as Intermediate, upper-intermediate and advanced students, often require less introductory work and greater pair or group-work, with the teacher moving from group to group providing individualized coaching as needed.

The Type of Student Group

As an example, many high schools throughout Japan place students in various academic levels according to the student's high-school entrance academic exam results, such as:

'T' Level - Technical or industrial minded students.

'S' Level - Standard or mainstream students, who are likely to progress into a junior college, technical school, or mainstream university.

'A' Level - Academically minded students, who are likely to progress to a more sort after university, and / or travel abroad for study.

'E' Level - Exemplary students exam focused toward entry into the best domestic schools or universities abroad.

The placement of students in any particular academic level does often reflect a general group dynamic or attitude toward learning and an overall interest in a particular subject, such as the learning of a second language.

Keeping all these factors in mind as you plan your lessons will assist you as you determine what time limits are required for each lesson component. As a general but flexible rule, there are four main components to a lesson. The following components and their suggested times reflect a common fifty-minute lesson. These time suggestions are:

Introduction, Warmer or Ice-breaker Activity
(5 to 10 minutes or 10 to 20 percent of the total lesson time).

Core Dialog or Concept Delivery
(15 to 20 minutes or 30 to 40 percent of the total lesson time).

Expanded Lesson, Practice or Reinforcement Activity
(15 to 20 minutes or 30 to 40 percent of the total lesson time).

Review and Assessment
(5 to 10 minutes or 10 to 20 percent of the total lesson time).

QUOTE:

"A teacher affects eternity: their influence immeasurable."

Henry Adams

Lesson Plan Formation

There are many different ways to format a lesson plan. Preference toward a particular style is a personal choice unless a certain formatted template is required by a governing organization. Most lesson plans will contain some, or all, of the following elements, which are typically in this order:

Title

The title for the lesson normally reflects the learning objective and context. Potential themes may include:

- Introductions
- In the neighborhood
- My living environment
- At the bus station
- Daily routines
- Life choices
- At the mall
- My birthday party

Objective

Two examples of how to write an objective are:

1. By the end of the lesson a student can..., or
2. At the end of the lesson a student will know...

Learning Environment (Lesson's Location)

Where will the lesson be conducted? Potential locations may include:

- In the classroom
- In the school's gym
- On the street corner
- At the park
- In a kitchen
- At the fire station

Materials

What materials will be needed to set the context and support all the lesson stages? Supporting materials may include:

- pictures or charts, real items (tangible objects such as stuffed animals), cooking supplies, etc.
- stationery (paper, crayons, colored pencils, glue, laminating sheets, tape, rubber-bands, paperclips, scissors, paper cutter, rulers, erasers, etc.).
- laptop computer, iPads or tablets, iPods or an MP3 player, digital projector, portable projector-screen, cables, speakers, CDs, portable cassette tape-decks or CD players, reading books, dictionaries, etc.
- Microsoft PowerPoint or Apple Keynote presentation software, a special context related guest, notes, handouts, attendance record book, class seating plan, student progress record files, board-games, etc.

Time

Each lesson's section should be assigned an approximate duration of time (for more detailed information see the section on *Lesson Timing*). Examples are:

1. Introduction, Warmer or Ice-breaker Activity - (5 to 10 minutes or 10 to 20 percent of the total lesson time).
2. Core Dialog or Concept Delivery - (15 to 20 minutes or 30 to 40 percent of the total lesson time).
3. Expanded Lesson, Practice or Reinforcement Activity - (15 to 20 minutes or 30 to 40 percent of the total lesson time).
4. Review and Assessment - (5 to 10 minutes or 10 to 20 percent of the total lesson time).

Introduction, Warmer or Icebreaker Activity

This is an activity component that focuses the student toward the lesson's context. This may include:

- showing photographs, images, graphs, real objects and / or playing context related games,
- watching a movie or music video, revision and / or previous lessons' concept practice,
- songs and / or chants,
- asking leading-questions,
- introducing a special context related guest.

Basic Lesson (Core Dialog) or Concept Delivery

This is an instructional component that describes the sequence of events that a teacher hopes will unfold as the lesson progresses. The content must relate to the central or most important part of the grammar or lesson concept being presented. This lesson element may contain:

- the setting of the current lesson's context,
- the teacher's instructional input and guided practice with the use of as many active learning tools as are suitable,
- delivery methods that target any or all of the English language skill areas, such as: listening, speaking, reading and / or writing,
- delivery methods that reinforce the student's learning through the student's senses, such as: hearing, sight, smell, taste, or touch.

Expanded Lesson, Practice or Reinforcement Activity

This is where expanding concepts can be practiced in groups, so long as each individual has an opportunity to develop personal skills in the area being presented. Practice is designed to reinforce and extend newly learned skills or knowledge, incorporating the important technique of peer teaching. This is where a teacher can:

- facilitate learning and assist students with the processing of new knowledge into long-term memory with various tools, such as the use of repetition and recall drills.

- to reinforce core structures, underlined variables are replaced. This will enable core dialog expansion. Examples are:

Question: What did you do on *the weekend*?
Variables: *the holidays*
your birthday
Monday
Response: I went to a movie.
Variables: *traveled to New Zealand*
stayed at home
went to school

Review and Assessment

A review component is delivered at the conclusion of the class period to wrap up the days lesson, to bring it all together. A passive assessment can also be undertaken to assess an individual's or student group's progress. This is usually conducted with a question and answer phase.

A short evaluation quiz can also be conducted at this time to ascertain whether adequate learning has occurred to a level of mastery expected by the teacher.

Analysis, Reflection, Modification (Being A.R.M.'d)

Now that the class session has concluded and data has been collected from observation, feedback, and assessments, the analysis component can begin. The teacher is now **A.R.M.**'d. This is where the teacher uses all the information available to reflect on the lesson itself—such as what worked when and how, what needs improving, what was the overall mood of the students, were the materials age-appropriate, were the lesson objectives met, were the times allotted for each component sufficient, what emotions were present during and after the lesson, etc.

A.R.M.'d with this knowledge, the teacher can now modify their approach and streamline their techniques for the future.

Table 48. General 50-Minute Lesson Plan Template

Lesson Title:			
Lesson's objective:			
Learning environment (Rationale)			
Component	**Description**	**Materials Required**	**Time**
Introduction, warmer or icebreaker activity			5 to **10** Minutes
Core dialog or concept delivery			**15** to 20 Minutes
Expanded lesson, practice or reinforcement activity			15 to **20** Minutes
Review and assessment			**5** to 10 Minutes
Analysis, Reflection, Modification (A.R.M.)			

QUOTE:

"The adjective is the banana peel of the parts of speech."

Clifton Paul Fadiman

✄ Setting Context ✄

By definition, *'context'* is a set of circumstances, conditions, or facts that form a relevant setting for an *event, situation, statement,* or *idea,* and in terms of which can give meaning to something, so that something can be fully understood.

It is commonly understood that many parts of speech, within a given language, depend on context (Auer, 1996). The setting of context within a classroom environment can be achieved in many ways. Some examples are:

Visual Aids

- The way a teacher dresses or the wearing of costumes,

- Arts and crafts, or real items, such as: a wall-clock or watch, stuffed-animals, books, a bike, a ball, or a lunch-box,

- Digital illustrations, such as: photos, graphs and charts, or any type of visual printed materials, as well as Microsoft PowerPoint or Apple Keynote presentations, Flickr slideshows, or digital books from iBooks or Kindle.

Video Aids

Commercially or personally produced DVDs, personally created videos, or YouTube videos.

The Internet and Social Media Tools

FaceBook, Twitter, Linkedin, MySpace, Google+, Flickr, YouTube or Ning.

Audio Aids

Teacher-teacher narratives (modeling), CDs, sound devices, such as: a radio, iPad tablet, iPod or MP3 player that are used as audio cues passively in the background, or for maximum focused effect played in the foreground.

Gestures

Charades or mime.

Once the context has been set successfully, then linking the context through modeling the appropriate and relevant target language can occur. Modeling should always progress toward student participation.

Student Profiling

Class atmosphere can be set by being at the classroom at least five minutes before the arrival of students. Greet each student personally as they arrive, preferably by name. Connections will be made and rapid positive rapport developed. The profiling of each student can also occur at this point.

On the first day of term, for each separate class, a teacher is unlikely to know each individual student's character. Over several weeks a new teacher will instinctively conduct passive profiling of their students, building rapport as they settle into their teaching routine. However, consistent focused daily profiling of each student as they first enter the classroom can be more empowering to the teacher, providing valuable information and clues to a student's attitude and relative current events.

The personal information collected during daily profiling of students can be extremely useful. The tidbits of information can be used to inject relevant comments toward an individual whose attention may have strayed making the lesson more relevant to them at a personal level.

As the teacher greets their students, they can also use this opportunity to:

- Observe and correct minor issues, such as bringing inappropriate materials or items to class.
- Check for untidy uniforms (if uniforms are worn), the chewing of gum, or the presence of food items that are likely to be consumed in the classroom during class time.
- Proactively calm boisterous or inappropriate behavior.
- Monitor individuals who may seem to have a justified or inappropriate mood that may be distracting to others.

Importance of Using Students' Names

It can be difficult for some teachers to memorize the names of all their students, especially if they teach 20 or more lessons a week with class-sizes of 30 to 40 students in each class. However, using a student's name during communication is one of the most effective ways of establishing a personal connection with that student, a tool to build positive rapport and maintain control.

One of the ways a teacher can remember the names of their students is to play name games. The following two name games are suggestions, best used at the beginning of any class or term:

1. The Name Chain.
2. The Name Association Game.

'The Name Chain'

1. Choose a topic, like favorite foods, hobbies, movies, or a musical entertainer or group. Write the appropriate corresponding dialog on the blackboard (writing surface). Examples are:

   Basic Model:

   > Hello. My name is _____ (e.g. John).
   > My favorite food is _____ (e.g. chocolate ice-cream).

   Expanded Model:

   > Hello. My name is _____ (e.g. John).
   > My favorite food is _____ (e.g. chocolate ice-cream), and my favorite movie is _____ (e.g. Star Wars).

2. The teacher and their students form a circle. The teacher leads-off by introducing the basic core dialog, such as:

   > Hello. My name is *Mr. Chris.*
   > My favorite food is *chocolate ice-cream.*

3. Student one then goes after the teacher, and says:

   > Hello. My name is *Yuki.* My favorite food is *Sushi.*
   > His name is *Mr. Chris.* His favorite food is *chocolate ice-cream.*

4. Student two then goes after the teacher and student one. They continue the process by saying:

   > Hello. My name is *Yuta.* My favorite food is *Udong noodles.*
   > His name is *Mr. Chris.* His favorite food is *chocolate ice-cream.*
   > Her name is *Yuki.* Her favorite food is *sushi.*

Continue the 'chain-like' process, restarting a new round when necessary, alternating the starting point with different students from the student formed circle.

QUOTE:

"Like everything metaphysical the harmony between thought and reality is to be found in the grammar of language."

Ludwig Wittgenstein

'The Name Association Game'

1. Each student must come up with an adjective that has a starting letter similar to the first letter in their name, such as:

   Compassionate Mr. Chris

2. Write the appropriate dialog on the blackboard as an example, such as:

   My name is _____ (e.g. compassionate) _____ (e.g. Mr. Chris).

The idea of this game is that each student must first say all of the names that came before him or her. The second person would say:

He is **compassionate** Mr. Chris, and I am *baby-face Jan*.

Alternatively, the teacher could have each student choose an animal, or any other category they find appropriate, beginning with the same letter as each student's first name, such as:

Robert the *R*accoon-dog, or **W**arren the *W*arrior-King

�֎ Gesture Assisted Learning �֎

One of the most common comments I have had on student feedback forms is that students appreciate and find gesturing essential for learning a second language. Over my many years of teaching, I have observed other teachers' use of gestures and have incorporated the best of them into my toolkit of tricks, as well as developing a set of gestures on my own that I use to direct and clarify what it is I want students to do. It is also important to use core dialog associated with each gesture consistently, and often repetitiously (X 3).

Gestures are an effective teacher / student communication tool for reinforcing unlearned language. Gestures are the first steps toward understanding and expressing a new language. It is unhelpful to discourage gesturing, but rather to encourage and include it as part of expressing any dialog. It is always better to be culturally sensitive and aware that gesturing in some cultures is not as prominent or acceptable as others (Italians often express themselves with gestures as a norm, whereas the Japanese are less likely to use them).

Students may not understand a teacher's style of gesturing over another's, when a teacher transition first occurs. The new teacher may experience hesitancy or confusion from his or her students at first. It is important to know that students will adapt and learn over time, so remember to always be consistent and patient.

Here are some effective gestures that are commonly used by many English language teachers (ELTs):

Listen to Me! Hand cupped behind the ear.

Bla Bla Bla. The fingers are held straight and together horizontally, with the thumb pointing downward, under the fingers. The thumb and fingers motion as if the hand is a 'head' and the thumb is its 'mouth'--suggesting a talking action. This is used to indicate that someone might be talking too much, is gossiping, or is boring, saying little that is relevant or of any consequence.

Stand up. Arms horizontally out to the side, palms up, and hands motioning upward.

Sit down. Arms horizontally out to the side, palms down, and hands motioning downward.

Pair up. On the first motion, show two fingers pointed up on one hand. On the second motion, bring both hands slowly together in front of the body, motioning the two students to come together [a soft clap].

Time Out! Use the sports *time-out* 'T' sign, using both hands forming a 'T'.

Stop! Use a hand stretched out in front of the body, palm-bent up toward the individual or group to be given the instruction to 'STOP'.

Good Job! Thumb up with other fingers forming a partial fist, or thumb and index finger forming a circle with the three other fingers pointing upward.

Congratulations!
Two people simultaneously raise one of their hands, palms facing each other, slapping hands together (a high-five).

*OK.** Connect the thumb and index-finger forming a circle with the three other fingers pointing upward.

Good Luck! Finger or fingers are crossed and shown to the person or persons who luck is given.

No or Not Right.
Either a slight shaking of the head from left to right, or a back-and-forth shaking of a pointed index finger directed toward the person or persons being communicating to.

Eliciting. A hand with slightly curved fingers in a horizontal position facing either up or down (dependent on the culture or country). The hand facing the recipient. The cupped hand beckoning the intent to have the person move forward toward the instructor.

Go Make a Phone-call, or You Have a Phone-Call.

The thumb and baby-finger, also known as the 'pinky', are outstretched with the other fingers tight against the palm. The thumb is placed next to the ear and the pinky placed next to the mouth, mimicking a telephone receiver.

Say That Again.

Hand in front of the body, arm stationary with the wrist and fingers rotating vertically, in a circular motion (like a wheel).

***Note:** A word of caution. Be culturally aware and sensitive. The gesture for the expression 'OK' means different things in different countries or cultures, as do many gestures. In the country of Japan the 'OK' gesture described above symbolizes 'money', but in parts of southern Europe and South America the gesture is seen as an obscene hand-gesture, often with the meaning of the recipient being perceived as an 'asshole.'

(see *Cross-cultural Awareness and Sensitivity*).

Warmers or Icebreakers

Warmers or Icebreakers are short five to ten minute focused activities that are usually introduced at the beginning of a lesson. By definition they:

- break ground*
- get one's feet wet*
- lay the first stone*
- lead the way*
- pave the way*
- set at ease*
- smooth the path* or smooth the way*
- start the ball rolling*

*Idioms: a set expression of two or more words whose meaning is not predictable from the literal meanings of its individual words.

Warmers are used for a variety of purposes. They are used to:

- allow the development and / or improvement of the student's listening, speaking, reading, and writing skills,
- review and practice known vocabulary or language structures,

- set the lesson's context and stimulate interest toward a topic, concept or the new language about to be delivered,
- reduce anxiety and build rapport,
- energize students toward predetermined objectives,
- initiate a change in the dynamics away from a teacher-led activity where the student (s) only watches and listens toward an active-learning model with a student's full sensory and emotional involvement,
- create a fun atmosphere so that students can learn and enjoy the use of new English language or expressions,
- model new language and express the use of intonation,
- show the link between expressing words and the use of body language to reinforce those words,
- stimulate creative thinking, and
- build self-confidence or foster cooperation and teamwork.

In the next section are a few warmer activities. These can be modified toward any level of student or student group:

Double Lines - 'Introductions'

First, write or display no more than five simple introduction sentences, either on the blackboard, whiteboard, or digitally projected. A suggested lesson could be about the question words: what, where, when, why, how, who, do, and which, etc. Examples of their use could be as follows:

1. What is your name?
2. Where do you go to school?
3. When is your birthday?
4. Why are you studying English?
5. How many subjects are you taking this year?
6. Who is your favorite musical group?
7. Do you have a nickname?
8. Which do you prefer, cold winters or hot summers?

Second, count-off all the students, such as: one, two, one, two, one, two, etc. Instruct the students who were assigned with the number 'one' to make the first line. Instruct the students who were assigned with the number 'two' to make a second line, facing the first line of students. Use gestures to reinforce the instructions. Each student should now be facing another.

Next, instruct line 'one' students to ask the line 'two' students the questions displayed, with line 'two' students answering, and vice-versa. Give an appropriate time for the majority of students to complete asking and answering the five questions. Once this has been accomplished, hands are clapped twice to cue line 'one' students to move right one-space, so that they are aligned with the next student in line 'two'. The student at the end of line 'one', who has been left without a line 'two' partner, should walk to the opposite end of their line, so that the lines are again even.

Don't be concerned if some students do not understand all instructions. Allow peer teaching to occur as students observe others and get involved. Also, use background music to set the mood of the activity; stopping the music to indicate that a position change is due. The position change will have to be modeled once or twice.

Teachers should only participate in an activity to reinforce the model. If a teacher does participate, they should quickly remove themselves from the activity as soon as possible and then go on with monitoring and motivating students as their priority.

'The Toilet Paper Game'

This game works best if the students are formed into a circle, with the students facing the center.

First, open a *new** roll of perforated toilet paper.

> ***Note:*** some students can be skittish about the use of a previously opened role of toilet paper [hygiene].

Second, instruct the students to take as many pieces of toilet paper as they like, from one piece to a maximum of 10 to 20 pieces. Make adjustments to the maximum potential pieces allowed, which is dependent on the English language level of the student being taught. The toilet-roll moves from one student to the next, with all students taking a turn to rip of their desired number of toilet paper sheets.

Next, once all the students have taken their desired number of toilet paper sheets, *only then* will the teacher give the final instructions, which is to give as many pieces of information about themselves as the number of squares they have taken from the toilet paper roll.

The teacher starts by giving their personal information, then continuing in a clockwise rotation to the next student until all students have had an opportunity to express their information, as required. Those students who struggle with providing the information can be assisted by other students as long as the student who is required to provide the information is involved in the process of learning the new language (peer teaching).

A variation to the use of toilet paper can be the use of candies / lollies, such as M & M's or individually wrapped salt-water-taffy.

'Paper Planes'

First, distribute one sheet of either standard A4 paper (210 × 297 mm or 8.3 × 11.7 in) or letter sized paper (8.5 by 11 inches or 215.9 mm × 279.4 mm) to all students. Have the students fold the paper in half, and then in half a second time, so that when opened, their paper has four sections. Have the students write a heading at the top of each of the four sections of their paper, choosing four headings from a list that has been displayed either on the blackboard, whiteboard, or digitally projected. Examples are:

1. Family or friends
2. Favorite color (s)
3. Food or drink
4. Hobby (s)
5. Nickname (s)
6. Sport (s)

Second, have the students write the answer to each section they have created, similar to what is shown in Diagram 3 below:

Figure 1. Paper Planes Worksheet Example

FAMILY	FOOD
I have one older brother. He is 17 years old. I have a younger sister. She is nine years old.	*My favorite food is Udong Noodles.*
FAVORITE COLOR	**HOBBIES**
blue.	*I enjoy computer games and playing baseball.*

Next, after the students have completed writing down their answers to each of the four sections, have them make a paper-plane (The teacher may have to model or provide a diagram of the making of a paper-plane).

Safety Instructions: Once all paper-planes have been created, have the students hold the paper-plane in one hand, while covering their eyes for protection with the other hand.

Next, instruct the students that music will soon begin to play. When they hear the music start, they are to throw their paper-plane above the heads of their fellow students, across the room. When the music stops they are to pick up the paper-plane closest to them. The music will then play again and the throwing of planes resumes. Continue this process six or seven times, ensuring the paper-planes are well distributed around the room and that it is less likely that the students will get their own paper-plane returned.

Next, at the conclusion of distribution, have the students select one paper-plane for themselves and pass on any other paper-plane to a student that has not received one. Then have all students open the paper-plane the possess and quietly read the information contained [to themselves].

Lastly, taking turns have the students read aloud the contents of their paper-plane and then have them try to guess whom the originator is. The student trying to guess who wrote the note can ask questions of individuals or the group, having responses limited to the raising or lowering of hands, or answering with a simple 'yes' or 'no' response.

Setting Context with 'Hidden Pictures'

Choose an image that relates to the context. Print it out as large as resources allow, or scan it into the digital presentation software (e.g. PowerPoint or Keynote). Only reveal this image to students 'after' they guess what it is by viewing a segment image that has been created from this original image as follows:

> **First**, to create the segment image, make sure that a segment is chosen that is not easily recognizable. Use an image editor, such as Photoshop. Crop the original image to a suitable segment and then enlarge that newly created segment.

> **Second**, the enlarged segment can be printed out on either a standard A4 paper (210 × 297 mm or 8.3 × 11.7 in) or letter sized paper (8.5 by 11 inches or 215.9 mm × 279.4 mm). It would be wise to prepare several context-related images using this same process.

Step one: Organize the students into cluster groups (four to six people).

Step two: The students are shown the segment image prompting a discussion toward guessing what the full image may be. As the students discuss the segment image, their ideas are written on the board. If the students are unable to guess what the full image is, after allowing time for pondering, then additional segment images may be given to trigger more thought and discussion toward guessing the correct full image.

✖ Blackboard Techniques ✖

The blackboard, or chalkboard [writing surface], is arguably the most important physical teaching aid available to an English language teacher (ELT). In third-world countries, the blackboard is the most readily available writing surface, but don't take the presence of a large writing surface for granted. In many lower socio-economic rural areas, schools may not even possess this basic luxury. In contrast, better-equipped schools may provide a whiteboard or digital whiteboard. Nevertheless, no matter what writing surface may be present, the principles on their use are the same.

The use of 'Chalk-and-Talk' with any curriculum continues to be a very effective method of teaching in most cultures. The blackboard is a visual tool that offers a variety of functions to an ESL teacher, so it is important that a teacher train himself or herself to use the blackboard effectively.

Here are some basic 'blackboard' techniques that will help in the delivery of content more effectively:

1. If a large blackboard or writing surface area is used, then divide the blackboard or writing surface into usable sections of approximately one-and-a-half meters square, either with lines or mentally.

2. Never write across the entire length of a large board. Write in straight horizontal lines. This is easy if a large blackboard or writing surface has been divided into sections as described above.

3. Use consistent font sizes for headings, subheadings, and text.

4. Writing should be large enough to read from the back of the class or at any angle. Keep in mind window glare.

5. Use white chalk on a blackboard as the primary color. Use a black whiteboard marker on a whiteboard as the primary color. Use different colored chalk and whiteboard markers to write or highlight important information.

   Caution: Some colors of chalk and whiteboard markers are difficult to see from a distance, or when light hits the writing surface through the windows or overhead lights. It is suggested that sample text is written on the writing surface, and checked from a distance.

6. Draw colored symbols, such as arrows, stars, shapes, or use call-outs, or write numbers next to text, to show the importance of information. Underline a single word or phrases to highlight a part of speech, or a variable.

7. The information that has been written on the blackboard or writing surface shouldn't be too crowded. Leave 'white space' [open space]. This assists students with ease-of-reading.

8. Only those items that need special and focused attention should be written on the blackboard or writing surface. Everything else can be verbalized, modeled, or discussed with students.

9. Never write on a blackboard or writing surface in script [*script*]. Students who have not been educated in Western countries, such as: Britain, Canada, Australia, New Zealand or the United States, have never seen script or hand writing. It will confuse them to introduce a new style of writing at the beginner to intermediate levels of English learning.

10. Write clearly and be consistent with letter-style choices. Many TESOL / TEFL teacher-trainees alter the use of letter-style when writing on the writing surface. This inconsistent writing confuses learners of a new language. In English, there are 52 characters in the English language alphabet (26 lower-case and 26 upper-case); excluding numeral characters. It's hard enough for false-beginners through elementary level students to learn and recall these, so why introduce a confusing variation?

11. More often than not, a teacher will unknowingly obstruct the blackboard or writing surface from their observing students, as they write with their back facing students. Another similar obstruction is when a teacher has finished writing, then turns and addresses the class obstructing the content on that surface with their body-mass and / or their gesturing. They should stand to the side and allow students to read or copy what has been written.

Furthermore, do not erase the board too quickly, as students need time to read and take-in new concepts and / or write down notes.

In addition, a teacher's back to their students, as they are writing on the blackboard or writing surface, may invite those who are looking for an opportunity to disrupt, to do so. It is difficult to manage the classroom when a teacher is unable to see what is going on behind them. A teacher should turn their head and body toward their students often, to maintain eye contact.

12. As a teacher 'prints' or draws on the blackboard or writing surface, they should say the words out loud simultaneously, or clearly describe what they are drawing, so that the students at the back of the classroom can more easily understand. This

technique has a double effect. First, students have differing learning styles; some students learn through observation, while others learn from both observation reinforced by listening.

Second, engaging students with oral dialog, as a teacher writes on the blackboard or writing surface, is more likely to keep their attention appropriately focused.

13. Class participation at the blackboard is a form of active learning. This technique keeps students alert and involved in their own learning. Invite students to participate from time to time.

❋ Drawing Effective Blackboard Stick-figures ❋

Inspiration for the writing of this segment has been drawn from the resource: **Andrew Wright (1984).** *1000+ Pictures for Teachers to Copy.* Addison Wesley Longman Ltd.,

I have owned a copy of Andrew Wright's book *1000+ Pictures for Teachers to Copy*, since 1998. I have used this book religiously over many years of global ESL teaching, with the same copy of the book being used by many of the hundreds of TESOL Teacher Trainees at my previously owned English language school and TESOL Teacher Training College, in New Zealand.

Simple stick figures drawn on the blackboard or writing surface will help to increase the interest of a lesson and are often a good tool to reinforce and give meaning to an idea, word, or phrase when uncertainty and / or confusion are apparent, or to convey intent. Stick figures should be line drawings, portraying only the most important details of the message.

Here are a few suggestions on how to use blackboard stick figures in the ESL classroom:

1. Use stick-figure drawings to build the context. This might also be helpful when a teacher wants to introduce a single word, phrase, concept, or core dialog. Stick-figure drawings can be used to introduce classroom rules at the beginning of the year, or to reinforce instructions for an upcoming activity.

2. A series or sequence of pictures would tell a visual story. Use the pictures as cues to encourage responses to questions.

3. It is important to draw quickly. The drawing itself should not be the center of attention, but rather to reinforce the main message being projected.

4. Drawings, especially faces that express emotions, should be drawn large enough to be seen from the back of the class.

5. Drawing is a tool that should be used sparingly.

�֍ Eliciting Individual Feedback ✤

Eliciting individual feedback is a common tool used to evoke or draw out an answer or obtain a response from a student, or group of students, in reaction to materials or information delivered that day, or at previous times, from a few days ago, a week, a term, or the previous year. It is a useful tool to assess individual or overall progress and levels of understanding.

Eliciting will get the students involved in the lesson, so that they pay more attention to what is being said or presented by the teacher, or others; keeping them on their toes. If the teacher has profiled their students at the beginning of the class (see student profiling), then that information can be used to inject and adjust the topic or the dialog *'on-the-fly'*, providing relevant student stimulation.

Eliciting individual feedback in itself is not teaching, but rather an assessment tool. Students that respond to this communication-trigger are only expressing what they have already learnt. However, their answers become a platform from which additional information can be delivered to increase knowledge. This later process is part of the learning process.

As students respond to elicitation they share ideas and hear new vocabulary from their teacher and from their peers. Peer-teaching occurs naturally making a teacher's job a little easier. This also provides an opportunity for the introduction of additional expanded vocabulary knowledge. New words or expressions can be recorded on the blackboard or writing surface, or written in student journals for deeper analysis at a later time.

✤ Background Music, Chants, and Songs ✤

Background Music in the Classroom

Music is a powerful tool for teaching the English language to speakers of other languages. Research has provided evidence that music has an affect on most living things: human beings, animals and even plants. Music, with a strong rhythm or beat, can stimulate brainwaves that can resonate in-sync with the beat; the faster the beats, the sharper the concentration. In contrast, a slower tempo promotes a calm meditative state.

Use *background music* to set the mood in the classroom or teaching space. Rauscher (1993) conducted research into the effects of music in the classroom, now known as *The Mozart Effect*. Rauscher observed students who had listened to *Mozart's Sonata for Two Pianos in D Major* for ten minutes before taking a test in spatial and abstract reasoning. The results showed that the subject students raised their scores significantly, compared to students who just listened to relaxation music or had silence (as cited in Jensen, 2000, pg. 246-247).

A study conducted by Nantais and Schellenberg, 1999 (cited in Jensen & Dabney, 2000) found that music stimulates the brain's right frontal lobe, which is where oral functioning, oral skills, planning, and social conduct occur. Jensen concludes,

> "The overall, positive effects of music on learning, such as activation and stimulation of the brain's limbic system, stress reduction, and increased molecular energy—all of what affect cognition and creativity—are well documented" (Jensen & Dabney, 2000, p. 78).

Music can contribute to a positive atmosphere in the classroom by creating a relaxed environment for study, or being upbeat and energized; both having the potential to enhance learning.

Brewer & Campbell (1991) suggest the following uses of music in the classroom:

- to create a relaxing atmosphere,
- to establish a positive learning state,
- to provide a multi-sensory learning experience that improves memory,
- to enhance active learning sessions,
- as background sound for learning activities,
- to increase attention by creating a short burst of energizing excitement,
- to release tension by using music with movement,
- to align groups,
- to develop rapport,
- to accentuate theme-oriented units,
- to provide inspiration, and
- to add an element of fun (p. 230).

Background music in the classroom stimulates the brain, reduces tension, and increases awareness. In my humble opinion and based on my experience, music used in the classroom by a teacher makes them *pretty cool*.

It might be debatable as to which music does what to students when; to either motivate them, stimulate increased targeted learning in them, or disrupt them. A teacher will know from their own observations and experience when to implement a trial and success model, to gauge best practice, or to avoid its use.

Chants

Participation in both *chants* and *songs* is a form of active learning. Both chants and songs are models of instruction that focus the responsibility of learning on the learner through active participation.

Research provides strong evidence that *chants*, also known as *stylized speech*, can be extremely beneficial in the English language learning process of nonnative speakers. The English language content being delivered to actively participating students, will encourage left-brain activity, while the use of repetitive rhythmic phrases in monotone, or reciting tones, vocalized in unison, will increase emotional processing and encourage and enhance right-brain activity. Stimulating the left and right brain functions simultaneously is said to maximize the student's ability to process information and retain that information in long-term memory.

Chants are used to expose and then reinforce common English language usage, in a rhythmic repetitive style. Chants also introduce the stress and intonation patterns that are associated with the English language.

Chants should accompany active physical participation when possible. This can be achieved by encouraging students to clap their hands, snap their fingers, stamp their feet, or strike an object on the table, to keep the rhythm of the chant. This is also fun!

Body movement can also accompany a chant to emphasize meaning. This works well with young-learners, but can also unleash the *'inner-child'* of some adult learners who may find this approach somewhat intimidating at first, but once they participate, they relax and have fun.

On the next page, *'The Description Chant'* with a second similar chant to the right called, *'The Shapes and Sizes Chant'* can have the content adjusted accordingly for young-learners, teenagers, or adults, dependent on the English language level of the student or student group.

QUOTE:

"We don't see things as they are, we see them as we are."

Anais Nin

Table 49. Chant Suggestions

The Description Chant (* Clap # Stomp Foot)	The Shapes and Sizes Chant (* Clap # Stomp Foot)
He's short. * *	It's tall. * * # * *
He's a short boy.	It's a tall tree.
He's tall. * *	It's little. * * # * *
He's a tall man.	It's a little bird.
----------	----------
She's young. * *	It's long. * * # * *
She's a young girl.	It's a long road.
She's old. * *	It's short. * * # * *
She's an old teacher.	It's a short dog.
----------	----------
Short boy. *	Tall tree. * *
Tall man. *	Little bird. * *
Young girl. *	Long road. * *
Old teacher. *	Short dog. * * # # *
----------	----------
He's thin. * *	It's round. * * # * *
He's a thin boy.	It's a round ball.
He's large. * *	It's square. * * # * *
He's a large teacher.	It's a square box.
----------	----------
Short boy. *	Tall tree. *
Tall man. * #	Little bird. * #
Young girl. *	Long road. *
Old teacher. * #	Short dog. * #
Thin boy. *	Round ball. *
Large teacher. * #	Square box. * * # * * # # * * # * * # #
Short boy. *	Tall tree. *
Tall man. * #	Little bird. * #
Young girl. *	Long road. *
Old teacher. * #	Short dog. * #
Thin boy. *	Round ball. *
Large teacher. * #	Square box. * * # * * # # * * # * * # #

Songs

Lake (2005) writes, "there is strong evidence supporting the use of music in the ESL classroom. Language and music are tied together in brain processing by pitch, rhythm and by symmetrical phrasing... Music can help familiarize students with connections and provides a fun way to acquire English."

Murphey (1992) conducted research looking at large corpus of pop song lyrics in relation to their affect on his ESL students learning the English language. He claims that a pattern emerged where the majority of songs had several linguistic features that he suggests would assist second-language learners of English, such as:

- There is a simple usage of English language words, with most lyrics written at an average of fifth-grade level.
- The language expressed is conversational, where imperatives and questions made up 25 percent of the sentences in the corpus.
- The lyrics are often sung at a rate slower than most people speak, with more pauses between utterances (allowing an increased absorption of new language).
- There is an abundance of repetition of the core dialog and their structures.

Murphey believed that these factors allow English language learners to comprehend better, learn their meanings and then they can relate better to the songs and the language used within them.

The practical use of songs in the classroom can be achieved by following these steps:

First, play a popular tune to students, once or twice, asking them to focus on the English lyrics.

Suggestions:

Elvis Presley	*Heartbreak Hotel*	(1956)
Bob Dylan	*Blowin' in the Wind*	(1963)
The Beatles	*Yesterday*	(1965)
	Yellow Submarine	(1969)
Dionne Warwick	*That's what friends are for*	(1985)
John Lennon	*Imagine*	(1971)
U2	*Beautiful Day*	(2000)
Jack Johnson	*3 Rs*	(2006)
James Blunt	*You're Beautiful*	(2006)

Second, distribute a handout to each of the students with the lyrics to the song. A number of key words should be missing (the target language). Choose words that complement the learning level objective.

Third, play the song two to three more times, allowing students to listen and then fill in the blanks. Pause at the conclusion of each round to receive feedback.

Next, provide the answers to the missing words, either orally, by writing on the blackboard or any writing surface, or by way of digital projector (using a presentation program), such as: PowerPoint or Keynote; remembering to spell-out each word once or twice.

Lastly, play the song a final time and let the students follow along, reading and listening as the song is played.

✖ Pair and Group-Work ✖

Pair and group-work is peer teaching, through interaction and practice - the *'doing'* element of acquiring a new language. Students will share skills with each other, one student being more skillful in one instance and the other being more skillful in another.

Students can interact with each other, which may seem a little less threatening than in a larger group dynamic, where many eyes are often watching the individual who is in the spotlight. Pair and group-work is where students can experiment with ideas, sharing, correcting, and adjusting as they express themselves, developing competence and confidence with the new language.

Pair and group-work also encourages students to become a little more outgoing because they are no longer sheltered, often hiding within a larger group. Pair and group work brings variety to lesson-time, allowing students to invest and personalize content, which raises personal interest and increases participation.

Vygotsky (1896 – 1934), a Russian psychologist, suggests that the upper limit of one's *Zone of Proximal Development (Z. P. D.)* is where a student can gain knowledge through interaction with a more skilled person (the lower limit of one's Z.P.D. is where limited independent learning occurs).

According to Vygotsky, *'Scaffolding'* occurs where there is a change in the level of support from a more skilled person who can articulate new ideas through dialog or other sensory delivery tools, during pair and / or group-work interactions. In a dialog, the persons' unsystematic, disorganized, and spontaneous ideas are met with the more systematic, logical and rational concepts of a more skilled or knowledgeable person, such as a peer or teacher.

To ensure that the lesson activities are linked to the lesson context, target language, and preplanned educational outcomes, preparation is essential and key to success. Clear instructions and expectations will reduce confusion, resistance and wasted time. Resources must be available and model-examples should be created for clarification. Physical models can be reused for future classes.

Group sizes, for best practice, are dependent on the activity; however, groups of two, four, six or eight are more manageable and facilitate inclusion of all members. Assigning students to groups can be random or self-assigned. They can also be created by counting out the students according to the number of groups the teacher intends to create, lining the students up or pointing to them one-at-a-time while seated, such as: one, two, three, four, five, six..., one, two, three, four, five, six..., one, two, three, four, five, six..., etc. and then asking students who were assigned with the number 'one', to go to table-one, students assigned with a number 'two', to go to table-two, 'three's to three, and so on. This technique usually separates students who are disruptive or divert attention away from the lesson tasks; however, it does not always work. If a student or students anticipate the teacher's technique, they may try to 'outfox' their teacher and pre-align themselves accordingly, in preparation. A teacher should always monitor their peripheral and be prepared to counter any distraction with another technique on the fly.

Another tactic is to formulate the group's makeup by asking predetermining questions before assigning students into groups. Examples are:

Who is a good motivator?

Who enjoys art?

Who is a good leader?

Who is creative?

Who has good writing skills?

Who is a chatterbox?

List each student on a blackboard or writing surface, assigning them according to a skill-area category. Assign one student from each category to a work-group, so that each work-group is represented by each skill-area.

A deck or pack of cards may also be useful. Shuffle the deck / pack and allow each student to draw a card. Once all students have drawn a card, assign a table or group using the cards: hearts table, spades table, clubs table and diamonds table (or any combination related to the deck / pack of cards).

All of these tactics and procedures provide an opportunity to introduce new vocabulary and phrases. Examples are:

If you have a _____ (e.g. queen of hearts), go to...

Students assigned the number _____ (e.g. 'one'), go to...

Note: During pair and group work, a teacher is freed to monitor all student group (s) and focus their attention toward students that are more in need, for both input and control. Allow and encourage independence and coach students toward becoming self-sustaining.

A teacher may be tempted to join in; however, the best thing that a teacher can do is to observe, monitor, and provide opinions as needed. A teacher should appreciate the learning that is taking place through their proactive facilitation!

QUOTE:

"I soon realized that no journey carries one far unless, as it extends into the world around us, it goes an equal distance into the world within."

Lillian Smith

Group Work (A One-Session Class)

A group activity is more commonly conducted during a one-session class. Here are a few suggestions:

'Crossword Creation'

This activity can be used to reinforce previously presented vocabulary, related to the current day's lesson. In this example 'transportation' vocabulary is used:

1. Organize students into pairs or small clusters of three to four persons.

2. Give each group a vocabulary list of about 10 to 15 words.

3. Have the students organize the words into a crossword formation (see Figure 2., left side).

4. Now have the students create cue questions for each word (see Figure 2., right side).

5. Students create a blank crossword puzzle to give to other students in other pair or cluster groups to solve.

Figure 2. Crossword Puzzle Example

Across

3 Aircraft with two pairs of wings, one above the othe

8 An aircraft with floats designed to land on water.

10 A small cart with a single wheel at the front.

12 A medium-sized sailboat equipped for cruising.

14 Used for sitting on.

Down

1 Two wheels held in a fram one behind the other.

2 A boat or ship that carries people or cars a short way

4 A silk cloth to help you dro from an aircraft.

5 A lightweight motorized bicycle.

6 A large vehicle carrying many passengers by road

7 A heavy armored fighting vehicle carrying guns.

9 A rubber covering on a wheel.

11 A horse-drawn cart with two or four wheels.

13 A narrow boat with pointec ends.

'What a Wonderful World'

The objective of this activity is to have students draw pictures illustrating the vocabulary they hear in the song, label it, and then discuss the drawings with classmates. The activity follows these steps:

1. Preparation:

    - Pay any fees and download the iTunes track 'What a Wonderful World,' a song written by Bob Thiele (as George Douglas) and George David Weiss; first recorded by Louis Armstrong (1968). Burn a CD if required.

    - Create picture cards that represent the vocabulary in the song's lyrics. They need to be big enough to be seen from the back of the classroom.

    - Ensure supplies are available, such as: CD player or a laptop with the means to play music over external speakers, markers and poster-paper.

2. Introduce the class to some basic Louis Armstrong facts:

    - a famous New Orleans, Louisiana jazz virtuoso trumpeter and singer / musician

    - born: August 4, 1901 – Louisiana, USA

    - died: July 6, 1971 – Queens, New York City, USA

    - his nickname was 'Satchmo' or 'Pops'

    - genres: Dixieland, jazz, swing, or traditional pop music

    - Grammy Award, 1964, Category: Male Vocal performance 'Hello Dolly'

    - 11 of his recordings have been inducted into the Grammy Hall of Fame

    - one of his recordings has been inducted into the Rock and Roll Hall of Fame

    - his home of 28 years (now a museum) was declared a National Historic Landmark in 1977

    - The New Orleans's Airport was renamed *Louis Armstrong International Airport* in his honor

3. Form the students into cluster-groups of 3 to 4 persons.

4. Inform the students that they are about to listen to one of Louis Armstrong's most famous songs, 'What a Wonderful World.' As they listen, they should think about the words of the song.

5. Direct the students to ponder then discuss, within their clusters, the following questions, to facilitate an upcoming class discussion:

   a. According to the song, what makes a wonderful world?
   b. What are the people doing in the song?
   c. What images come to mind when listening to the song (colors, shapes, textures, etc.)?

6. Facilitate a class discussion while reviewing key vocabulary from the song and presenting picture-cards prepared earlier. The students should be encouraged to provide comparison statements on the contents of the song and the picture-cards that were displayed. Write the words or phrases students express on the blackboard or writing surface.

7. Provide poster-paper to each student cluster group, then instruct them to listen to the song a few times. As they listen they should create a poster of the images they have envisioned related to the Louis Armstrong song, 'What a Wonderful World.'

   Note: Playing the song too much may become bothersome.

8. Instruct the students to label the poster's individual images with as much appropriate English vocabulary as time allows.

9. Allow enough time before the conclusion of the class for the students to share their work with their peers, having each student cluster group stand one-by-one and give a short presentation of their work.

10. The students can choose their favorite poster, with interactive class discussion accompanying the decision process. This should conclude the session.

'That's My Line'

That's my line is used at the conclusion of the class session. First, there are a few preceding activities to conduct, building up to the 'That's my line' finale.

1. Preparation:

   • Pay any fees and download the iTunes track 'Imagine,' a song written by John Winston Lennon (or any other suitable song). *Imagine* is the first track on his album of the same name, released in 1971.

   • Create lyric work-sheets for each student. Ensure that 10 to 20 key-words are missing throughout the lyrics with an underline inserted in each missing word's place.

- Ensure supplies are available, such as scissors and a CD player or a laptop with the means to play music over external speakers.

2. Form the students into cluster-groups of 3 to 4 persons.

3. Instruct the students that they should read and listen to the song's English words as it plays, filling in the missing words as they hear them. Play the song two or three times if necessary.

4. Provide the answers for the missing lyrics, eliciting answers from different individuals.

5. Once all the answers have been written into the blanks, play the song again with the students reading their completed lyrics in unison with the song.

6. Assign one verse from the song to each student cluster-group. Have a member from each group cut the assigned verse's lyrics into one-sentence lines.

7. Play the song again, but this time, have each student line up, in the correct order as the lyrics they are holding are played. It may take a few tries to get it right.

   As an alternative to creating a line-up, have the students stand up as the line in the student's possession is sung, or have them put up their hand.

Group Work (Multi-Session Classes)

A group activity can be conducted over multiple-sessions. Here are a few suggestions:

Vocabulary Flashcard Creation

Flashcards bear information such as images, symbols, letters, vocabulary or numbers, on either one or both sides. English language teachers (ELTs) and their students use flashcards for drills or individual study to aid memorization by way of *spaced repetition*. On one side of the card a prompt is placed, to trigger a response. Usually, the response or answer is placed on the other side of the card.

A teacher can spend hours creating several sets of flashcards or use personal funds buying them. If resources allow, get the students to create their own sets of flash-cards. The process of creating, coloring, writing, reviewing and correcting content before their creations are laminated for durability, will assist in their learning and retention. The flashcards become invaluable tools for study or can be used to conduct assessments such as term or year-end exams.

Communicative Board Game Creation

Board or card games have been stereotypically labeled and used as merely fillers, time-killers, and a lazy tool to 'babysit' English language learners in the ESL classroom. However, research backs the use of educational games to teach English to speakers of other languages and suggests that the use of carefully selected board or card games are invaluable and should be an important part of any English language learning curriculum.

Board and card games are a welcome break from highly stressful routines, found in most schools. Board or card games facilitate English language learning by creating an atmosphere whereby students relax and have focus where they become highly motivated. Students passively, as well as actively, listen. They interact with each other, communicate, and are usually completely unaware that language learning is taking place. Board and card games are effective and fun, and develop class cohesion, are student-centered, promote healthy competition, and provide meaningful context in which all language skills can be observed, practiced, and developed.

Take the playing of English language board and card games in the ESL classroom a step further. Don't just play commercially made games—get the students to create their own personalized board or card games.

Set some guidelines for the game's creation. Examples are:

1. The game must have a suitable context.

2. The objective - to increase knowledge of the English language.

3. The size of the final laminated game board (A3 size 420 x 297 mm or 16.5 x 11.7 in), or individually laminated playing cards (no larger than an A6 size 148 x 105 mm or 5.8 x 4.1 in).

4. To also create all game pieces needed, such as: die or dice, money, coins, tokens, question cards or the game's player pieces, etc.

5. The number of players (four to six students, or a group-game).

6. A playing time limit (30 to 50 minutes).

7. A project time limit to include testing within the creator's group and to exchange with another group in the class for testing so peer feedback can be gathered and then adjustments made by the creators (four to six 50-minute sessions).

8. To produce one set of English instructions (rules) and one set of instructions (rules) in their native language.

Write on the blackboard or writing surface a few useful English gaming expressions that can be used in their game. Examples are:

move back 5 spaces	miss a turn	pay $200.00 tax
move forward 3 spaces	pickup a card	go back to start

Provide the materials needed, organize the students into groups (four to six students in each group), and then let the creativity from the students naturally bubble over. Learning English should be fun and introducing a 'game creation' session or sessions into the year's curriculum can trigger excitement and interest.

Once the games are complete, have the students play and evaluate each other's creations using simple evaluation sheets, judging which creation meets predetermined criteria, such as having a focus on learning the English language, being fun, and fits a time requirement (ten-minutes to forty-minutes, etc.).

Prizes can be offered for the best creation. It can become an annual interclass activity, where several classes at the same or at different levels compete to create the best English language board game.

QUOTE:

"It is not the answer that enlightens, but the question."

Eugene Lonesco

APPENDIX

TEACHER RESOURCES

Dialogs and Role-plays

Table 50. Dialog Practice Suggestions for Various Contexts

Context	Purpose	Suggested Language
Introductions	Expressing personal information Finding out more information about other people	A: What's your name? B: My name is Mr. Chris, your English teacher. A: Where are you from? B: I'm from the United States. ***Expanded Dialog:*** A: Where do you live? B: I live in Yokohama City, near Tokyo.
Daily Routine	Asking about another person's activities	A: What time do you start school? B: I start school at 08:30. A: What time do you eat lunch? B: I eat lunch from 12:30 to 13:00. ***Expanded Dialog:*** A: What do you eat for lunch? B: I like to eat sandwiches for lunch.

Context	Purpose	Suggested Language
In the Neighborhood	Asking and receiving directions Asking distance	A: Where can I find the bank? B: The bank is next to McDonalds. A: Where is the bakery? B: The bakery is across from the bar. ***Expanded Dialog:*** A: How far is the library? B: Only about ten minutes on foot.
Job Interview	Introducing yourself Responding to questions directed at you	A: Good morning. What's your name? B: My name is Christopher from Yokohama. A: What position would you like? B: I'm interested in administration. ***Expanded Dialog:*** A: Do you have any experience? B: Yes, I do. I worked for the University of Tokyo for 15 years.
At the Mall	Getting instructions	A: Where can I buy a digital HD TV? B: You can buy a digital HD TV at the home-center. A: Where is the home-center? B: The home-center is next to McDonalds restaurant. ***Expanded Dialog:*** A: Is the home-center open on the weekend? B: Yes! The home-center is open from 08:00 to 18:00.

Context	Purpose	Suggested Language
At the Train Station At the Travel Agent	Getting and giving information Asking the price Buying a ticket Information clarification	A: What time does <u>the express train</u> depart from <u>New York</u> to <u>Chicago</u>? B: <u>The express train</u> for <u>Chicago</u> departs <u>daily</u> at <u>08:00</u>. A: How much is a one-way ticket? B: A one-way ticket costs <u>$78.00</u>. A: How much is a round-trip ticket? B: A round-trip ticket costs <u>$139.00</u>. ***Expanded Dialog:*** A: I'll have a round-trip ticket departing on <u>November 21</u> and returning on <u>December 25</u>, please. A: Where does the train leave from? B: The express train for <u>Chicago</u> leaving on <u>November 21</u>, at <u>08:00</u> departs from <u>platform 2</u>.
The Weather	Getting weather information	A: What do you think the weather will be like <u>tomorrow</u>? B: It will be <u>cloudy</u>. A: What do you think the weather will be like <u>this weekend</u>? B: It will be <u>sunny and warm</u>. ***Expanded Dialog:*** A: Should I bring <u>a coat</u>, just in case? B: Yes! <u>You should wear layered clothing in this environment</u>.

Context	Purpose	Suggested Language
At a Restaurant	Talking about food Ordering	A: What are you going to order? B: I'll have <u>a hamburger-steak</u>. A: I'm going to have <u>the fried rice</u>. A: What would you like to drink? B: I'll have <u>a diet coke</u>. A: I'll just have <u>some ice-water</u>. ***Expanded Dialog:*** C: May I take your order? B: Yes, please! I'll have <u>a hamburger-steak</u> and my friend will have <u>the fried rice</u>. C: Would you like anything to drink? A: Yes, please! My friend will have <u>a diet coke</u> and we'll both have some <u>ice-water</u>. Thank you!
Living Environment	Making choices Describing activities	A: Where would you like to live? B: I'd like to live in the <u>country</u>! A: Why do you like the <u>country</u>? B: Because I like <u>nature</u>, <u>open spaces</u> and <u>fresh air</u>. ***Expanded Dialog:*** A: What can you do in the <u>country</u>? B: You can <u>go fishing</u> or <u>hike in the mountains</u>.
School Life	Expressing your interests	A: How's your school life going? B: It's OK, but I'm thinking <u>about joining a sport's club</u>. A: What are you interested in? B: I like <u>tennis</u>!

List of Irregular Verbs

Table 51. Irregular Verbs

Irregular Verbs			3rd Person Singular	Present Participle / Gerund (–ing form)
Base Form	Past Simple	Past Participle		
abide	abode abided	abode abided abidden	abides	abiding
alight	alit / alighted	alit / alighted	alights	alighting
arise	arose	arisen	arises	arising
awake	awoke	awoken	awakes	awaking
be	was / were	been	is	being
bear	bore	born / borne	bears	bearing
beat	beat	Beaten / beat	beats	beating
become	became	become	becomes	becoming
begin	began	begun	begins	beginning
behold	beheld	beheld	beholds	beholding
bend	bent	bent	bends	bending
bet	betted / bet	betted / bet	bets	betting
bid	bade / bid	bidden / bid	bids	bidding
bid	bid	bid	bids	bidding
bind	bound	bound	binds	binding
bite	bit	bitten / bit	bites	biting
bleed	bled	bled	bleeds	bleeding
blow	blew	blow / blowed	blows	blowing
break	broke	broken	breaks	breaking
breed	bred	bred	breeds	breeding
bring	brought	brought	brings	bringing
broadcast	broadcast broadcasted	broadcast broadcasted	broadcasts	broadcasting

build	built	built	builds	building
burn	burnt burned	burnt burned	burns	burning
burst	burst	burst	bursts	bursting
bust	bust / busted	bust / busted	busts	busting
buy	bought	bought	buys	buying
cast	cast	cast	casts	casting
catch	caught	caught	catches	catching
choose	chose	chosen	chooses	choosing
clap	clapped clapt	clapped clapt	claps	clapping
cling	clung	clung	clings	clinging
clothe	clad / clothed	clad / clothed	clothes	clothing
come	came	come	comes	coming
cost	cost / costed	cost / costed	costs	costing
creep	crept	crept	creeps	creeping
cut	cut	cut	cuts	cutting
dare	dared / durst	dared	dares	daring
deal	dealt	dealt	deals	dealing
dig	dug	dug	digs	digging
dive	dived / dove	dived	dives	diving
do	did	done	does	doing
draw	drew	drawn	draws	drawing
dream	dreamt dreamed	dreamt dreamed	dreams	dreaming
drink	drank	drank / drunk	drinks	drinking
drive	drove	driven	drives	driving
dwell	dwelt dwelled	dwelt dwelled	dwells	dwelling
eat	ate	eaten	eats	eating
fall	fell	fallen	falls	falling
feed	fed	fed	feeds	feeding

feel	felt	felt	feels	feeling
fight	fought	fought	fights	fighting
find	found	found	finds	finding
fit	fit/fitted	fit/fitted	fits	fitting
flee	fled	fled	flees	fleeing
fling	flung	flung	flings	flinging
fly	flew / flied	flown / flied	flies	flying
forbid	forbade forbad	forbidden forbad	forbids	forbidding
forecast	forecast forecasted	forecast forecasted	forecasts	forecasting
foresee	foresaw	foreseen	foresees	foreseeing
foretell	foretold	foretold	foretells	foretelling
forget	forgot	forgotten	forgets	forgetting
forgive	forgave	forgiven	forgives	forgiving
forsake	forsook	forsaken	forsakes	forsaking
freeze	froze	frozen	freezes	freezing
frostbite	frostbit	frostbitten	frostbites	frostbiting
get	got	got/gotten	gets	getting
give	gave	given	gives	giving
go	went	gone	goes	going
grind	ground	ground	grinds	grinding
grow	grew	grown	grows	growing
handwrite	handwrote	handwritten	handwrites	handwriting
hang	hung hanged	hung hanged	hangs	hanging
have	had	had	has	having
hear	heard	heard	hears	hearing
hide	hid	hidden / hid	hides	hiding
hit	hit	hit	hits	hitting
hold	held	held	holds	holding

hurt	hurt	hurt	hurts	hurting
inlay	inlaid	inlaid	inlays	inlaying
input	input inputted	input inputted	inputs	inputting
interlay	interlaid	interlaid	interlays	interlaying
keep	kept	kept	keeps	keeping
kneel	knelt kneeled	knelt kneeled	kneels	kneeling
knit	knit / knitted	knit / knitted	knits	knitting
know	knew	known	knows	knowing
lay	laid	laid	lays	laying
lead	led	led	leads	leading
lean	leant leaned	leant leaned	leans	leaning
leap	leapt leaped	leapt leaped	leaps	leaping
learn	learnt learned	learnt learned	learns	learning
leave	left	left	leaves	leaving
lend	lent	lent	lends	lending
let	let	let	lets	letting
lie	lay	lain	lies	lying
light	lit / lighted	lit / lighted	lights	lighting
lose	lost	lost	loses	losing
make	made	made	makes	making
mean	meant	meant	means	meaning
meet	met	met	meets	meeting
melt	melted	molten melted	melts	melting
mislead	misled	misled	misleads	misleading
mistake	mistook	mistaken	mistakes	mistaking
mis-understand	mis-understood	mis-understood	mis-understands	mis-understanding

mow	mowed	mown mowed	mows	mowing
overdraw	overdrew	overdrawn	overdraws	overdrawing
overhear	overheard	overheard	overhears	overhearing
overtake	overtook	overtaken	overtakes	overtaking
pay	paid	paid	pays	paying
preset	preset	preset	presets	presetting
prove	proved	proven proved	proves	proving
put	put	put	puts	putting
quit	quit / quitted	quit / quitted	quits	quitting
read	read	read	reads	reading
rid	rid ridded	rid ridded	rids	ridding
ride	rode / rid	ridden	rides	riding
ring	rang	rung	rings	ringing
rise	rose	risen	rises	rising
rive	rived	riven rived	rives	riving
run	ran	run	runs	running
saw	sawed	sawn / sawed	saws	sawing
say	said	said	says	saying
see	saw	seen	sees	seeing
seek	sought	sought	seeks	seeking
sell	sold	sold	sells	selling
send	sent	sent	sends	sending
set	set	set	sets	setting
sew	sewed	sewn / sewed	sews	sewing
shake	shook	shaken	shakes	shaking
shave	shaved	shaven shaved	shaves	shaving
shear	shore sheared	shorn sheared	shears	shearing
shed	shed	shed	sheds	shedding

shine	shone shinned	shone shinned	shines	shining
shoe	shod	shod	shoes	shoeing
shoot	shot	shot	shoots	shooting
show	showed	shown showed	shows	showing
shrink	shrank shrunk	shrunk shrunken	shrinks	shrinking
shut	shut	shut	shuts	shutting
sing	sang	sung	sings	singing
sink	sank sunk	sunk sunken	sinks	sinking
sit	sat	sat	sits	sitting
slay	slew / slayed	slain / slayed	slays	slaying
sleep	slept	slept	sleeps	sleeping
slide	slid	slid slidden	slides	sliding
sling	slung	slung	slings	slinging
slink	slunk	slunk	slinks	slinking
slit	slit	slit	slits	slitting
smell	smelt smelled	smelt smelled	smells	smelling
sneak	sneaked snuck	sneaked snuck	sneaks	sneaking
sow	sowed	sown sowed	sows	sowing
speak	spoke spake	spoken	speaks	speaking
speed	sped speeded	sped speeded	speeds	speeding
spell	spelt spelled	spelt spelled	spells	spelling
spend	spent	spent	spends	spending
spill	spilt spilled	spilt spilled	spills	spilling

spin	span spun	spun	spins	spinning
spit	spat spit	spat spit	spits	spitting
split	split	split	splits	splitting
spoil	spoilt spoiled	spoilt spoiled	spoils	spoiling
spread	spread	spread	spreads	spreading
spring	sprang sprung	sprung	springs	springing
stand	stood	stood	stands	standing
steal	stole	stolen	steals	stealing
stick	stuck	stuck	sticks	sticking
sting	stung	stung	stings	stinging
stink	stank / stunk	stunk	stinks	stinking
stride	strode	stridden	strides	striding
strike	struck	struck stricken	strikes	striking
string	strung	strung	strings	stringing
strip	stript stripped	stript stripped	strips	stripping
strive	strove strived	striven strived	strives	striving
sublet	sublet	sublet	sublets	subletting
sunburn	sunburned sunburnt	sunburned sunburnt	sunburns	sunburning
swear	swore	sworn	swears	swearing
sweat	sweat sweated	sweat sweated	sweats	sweating
sweep	swept sweeped	swept sweeped	sweeps	sweeping
swell	swelled	swollen swelled	swells	swelling
swim	swam	swum	swims	swimming
swing	swung	swung	swings	swinging

take	took	taken	takes	taking
teach	taught	taught	teaches	teaching
tear	tore	torn	tears	tearing
tell	told	told	tells	telling
think	thought	thought	thinks	thinking
thrive	throve thrived	thriven thrived	thrives	thriving
throw	threw	thrown	throws	throwing
thrust	thrust	thrust	thrusts	thrusting
tread	trod	trod / trodden	treads	treading
undergo	underwent	undergone	undergoes	undergoing
understand	understood	understood	understands	understanding
undertake	undertook	undertaken	undertakes	undertaking
upset	upset	upset	upsets	upsetting
wake	woke waked	woken waked / woke	wakes	waking
wear	wore	worn	wears	wearing
weave	wove weaved	woven weaved	weaves	weaving
wed	wed wedded	wed wedded	weds	wedding
weep	wept	wept	weeps	weeping
wet	wet wetted	wet wetted	wets	wetting
win	won	won	wins	winning
wind	wound winded	wound winded	winds	winding
withdraw	withdrew	withdrawn	withdraws	withdrawing
withhold	withheld	withheld	withholds	withholding
withstand	withstood	withstood	withstands	withstanding
wring	wrung	wrung	wrings	wringing
write	wrote / writ	written / writ	writes	writing

Table 52. Abbreviations Common in English

A

a.	adjective (in early volumes)	adj.	adjective
adv.	adverb	adv. phr.	adverb phrase
Amer.	American	Amer. Eng.	American English
app.	Appendix	applic.	application
Aug.	August	AU	Australia
AT	Austria	aux. v.	auxiliary verb

C

CA	Canada	c.	century
c.	Chapter (reference)	coll.	college
concr.	concrete	conj.	conjunction
const.	constructed with	corresp.	correspondence

D

Dan.	Danish	Dec.	December
def. art.	definite article	demonstr.	demonstrative
demonstr. adj.	demonstrative adjective	demonstr. pron.	demonstrative pronoun
det.	determiner	DK	Denmark
dial.	dialect	Du.	Dutch

E

early ME	early Middle English	Eccl. L.	Ecclesiastical Latin
Eccl.	Ecclesiastes	eccl.	ecclesiastic (al)
Ed.	edition, editor	Ed. *or* ed.	Education
EG	Egypt	ellipt.	elliptical
Eng.	England; English	equiv. to	equivalent to
esp.	especially	etc.	et cetera

F

FJ	Fiji	FI	Finland
FR	France	F.	French
Feb.	February	fem.	feminine / female
f.n.	footnote	F. / Fri.	Friday

G

Gael.	Gaelic (Scots)	gen.	General (-ly)
Germ.	German	DE	Germany
GK / Gk	Greek	Glos.	Glossary
GR	Greece	GL	Greenland

I

imper. imp. impv.	imperative	indef.	indefinite
indef. art.	indefinite article	inf. / infin.	infinitive
infl.	inflected, inflection	int. / interj.	interjection
Inter'l Int.	International	interrog. pron.	interrogative pronoun
intr.	intransitive	intrans.	intransitive
intro. introd.	introduction introduce	IE	Ireland
Ir.	Irish / Ireland	irreg.	irregular
IL	Israel	It.	Italian / Italy
IT	Italy	IT	Information Technology

J

Jan.	January	JP	Japan

L

L.	Latin	late L.	late Latin
LG	Low German	l. L.	Late Latin
L. / Lon.	London	lit.	Literal (-ly) / literature

M

MY	Malaysia	marg.	margin
masc.	masculine	M. / Mon.	Monday

N

NP	Napal	NL	Netherlands
n.	noun / note / name / new / national		
n. phr.	noun phrase	n. pl.	noun plural
Nat.	National	N. Isl.	North Island
north.	northern	Nov.	November
No. num.	Numeral (-s)	N.Z. (NZ)	New Zealand Aotearoa
NO	Norway	—	—

O

obs.	obsolete	occas.	occasionally
Oct.	October	OE	Old English
OED	Oxford English Dictionary	orig.	original

P

p.	paragraph / part / participle / person / past / population		
p. / pp.	page	pers. pron.	personal pronoun
Pg.	Portuguese	phr.	phrase(s)
pl.	place	plur.	plural
possess.	possessive	Pos.	positive
p.p.	past participle	possess. pron.	possessive pronoun
pref.	preface	p. adj.	participle adjective
prep.	preposition	pref.	prefix
pres. t.	present tense	pres. p.	present participle
pr. / pron.	pronoun	prop. n.	proper noun

Q

QA	Qatar	quot.	quotation

R

refl. / reflex.	Reflexive	reflex. pron.	reflexive pronoun
rel. pron.	relative pronoun	rh.	rhyming with

S

Sat.	Saturday	Scand.	Scandinavian
Sept. Sep.	September	Shak.	Shakespeare
sing.	singular	SG	Singapore
ZA	South Africa	KR	Republic of *South Korea*
ES	Spain	spec.	specialized
spec. specif.	special specifically	subjunct.	subjunctive
sup. superl.	superlative	SE	Sweden
Sw.	Swedish	CH	Switzerland
sub. subj.	subject	Suf. / Suff.	Suffix

T

TW	Taiwan	TH	Thailand
Th. / Thur.	Thursday	trans.	transitive
transf.	Transfer transferred	transl.	translate translation
T. / Tue.	Tuesday	TR	Turkey

U

AE	United Arab Emirates	GB	United Kingdom
US	United States	VN	Veitnam

V

v.	verb	var.	variant
vbl. n.	verbal noun	verb. prefix	verbal prefix
verb. phr.	verbal phrase	v.r.	variant reading

W

W. / Wed.	Wednesday	W.	West, Wales, Welsh

196

Table 53. International Phonetic Alphabet

Vowels							
Monophthongs				Diphthongs			
i: tree seat	ɪ sit fish	ʊ good put	u: food shoe	ɪəʳ fear beer	eɪ eight they	—	
e bet head	ə about cinema	ɜ:ʳ girl learn	ɔ: door call	ʊə tourist pure	ɔɪ toy choice	əʊ throw joke	
æ apple black	ʌ cup love	ɑ: father heart	ɒ stop rock	eəʳ where chair	aɪ thigh eye	aʊ lounge cow	
Consonants							
p apple pet	b about bad	t time tea	d door lady	tʃ check church	dʒ large lounge	k walk cat	g green flag
f fish food	v voice five	θ think earth	ð they mother	s stop fast	z lazy noise	ʃ shoe crash	ʒ vision casual
m money lemon	n nurse green	ŋ English sing	h hello heart	l little pull	r red tree	w wind wet	j yellow year

REFERENCES

Auer, P. (1996). On the prosody and syntax of turn-continuations. In Elizabeth Couper-Kuhlen and Margaret Selting, eds., *Prosody in Conversation: International Studies*, 57-100. Cambridge: Cambridge University Press.

Brewer, C., & Campbell, D. (1991). *Rhythms of learning*. Tucson, Arizona: Zephyr Press.

Bonwell, C., & Eison, J. (1991). *Active learning: Creating excitement in the classroom*. ASHE-ERIC Higher Education Report No. 1. Washington, D.C.: The George Washington University.

Boothman, N. (2000). *How to Make People Like You in 90 Seconds or Less*. New York, NY: Workman.

Bunting, (2004). Secondary schools designed for a purpose; but which one? *Teacher*, No. 154, 10-13.

Chickering, A, & Gamson, Z., (1987). Seven principles for good practice in undergraduate education. *American Association of Higher Education Bulletin,* 39(7), 3-7.

Doff, A. (1990). *Teach English: A training course for teachers. Teacher's handbook*. Cambridge: Cambridge University Press.

Fuzzimo. Cover Design Element (a free downloadable pack of vector post-it notes and drawing-pins), extracted on 29th March 2012. http://www.fuzzimo.com/free-vector-post-it-notes-push-pins/

Gralnick, J. (n.d.). *Half of U.S. homes own Apple products*. USA Today / Tech. Retrieved June 21, 2012, from: http://www.usatoday.com/tech/news/story/2012-03-28/cnbc-survey-apple-products-us-homes/53827254/1 (Posted 3/28/2012 12:29 PM l Updated 3/28/2012 1:26 PM)

Howell, W. (1982). *The empathic communicator*. Belmont, CA: Wadsworth.

Jensen, E. (2000, Nov.) "Moving with the Brain in Mind" Educational Leadership, 58(3), 34-38.

Jensen, E., & Dabney, M. (2000). Learning smarter. San Diego: The Brain Store.

King Jr., M. L. (1958). *Stride toward freedom: The Montgomery story.* New York, NY: Harper.

Lake, B. (2005). Music and language learning. *ESL Journal*, 22(5), 33-42.

Lowman, J. (1984). *Mastering the Techniques of Teaching.* San Francisco: Jossey-Bass.

McKeachie, W. J., Pintrich P., Lin Y., & Smith D. (1986). Teaching and learning in the college classroom: A review of the research literature. Arbor A.: *Regents of The Univ. of Michigan*. Ed. 314 999, 124 pp.

Murphey, T. (1992). The discourse of pop songs. *TESOL Quarterly*, 26(4), 770-774.

Nantais, K. M., & Schellenberg, E. G. (1999). The Mozart effect: An artifact of preference. *Psychological Science*, 10, 370-373.

Rauscher F., Shaw G., (1993). Music and spatial task performance. *Nature*, 365: 611 pp.

Richards, J. C. and Rodgers T. S. (1986). *Approaches and methods in language teaching: A description and analysis.* Cambridge: Cambridge University Press.

Ruhl, K., Hughes, C., & Schloss, P. (1987, Winter). Using the pause procedure to enhance lecture recall. *Teacher Education and Special Education,* 10, 14-18.

Swan, M. (1997). *Practical English Usage.* Oxford, Oxford University Press.

Thornbury, S. (2005). Dogme: Dancing in the Dark? *Folio.* 9/2, 3-5.

Spielberg, S. A., et al. (Producer), & Spielberg, S. A. (Director). (1985). *The Color Purple.* United States: Amblin Entertainment: Warner Bros. Pictures.

RECOMMENDED BOOKS and READINGS

Brown, J. (1995). *The Elements of Language Curriculum.* Boston, MA: Heinle and Heinle.

Chambers, F. (1997). Seeking consensus in course-book evaluation. *English Language Teaching Journal*, 51(1), 29-35.

Clarke, D. (1991). The negotiated syllabus: What is it and how is it likely to work? *Applied Linguistics*, 12(1), 13-28.

Cunningsworth, A. (1984). *Evaluating and Selecting EFL Teaching Materials.* London: Heinemann.

Dubin, Fraida, Olshtain, & Elite (1986). *Course Design: Developing Programs and Materials for Language Learning.* Cambridge: Cambridge University Press.

Ellis, & Rod (1993). The empirical evaluation of language teaching materials. *English Language Teaching Journal*, 51(1), 36-42.

Eken, D. (1996). Ideas for using songs in the English language classroom. *English Teaching Forum*, 34 (1), 46-47.

Grant, N. (1987). *Making the Most of your Textbook.* London: Longman.

Griffee, D. (1990). Hey baby! Teaching short and slow songs in the ESL classroom. *TESL Reporter*, 23(4), 3-8.

Griffiths, C. (1995). Evaluating materials for teaching English to adult speakers of other languages. *Forum*, 33(3), 50-51.

Henrichsen, L. (1983). Teacher preparation needs in TESOL: The results of an international survey. *RELC Journal*, 14(1), 18-45.

Hutchinson, T., & Waters, A. (1987). *English for Specific Purposes.* Cambridge: Cambridge University Press.

Hutchinson, T., & Torres, E. (1994). The textbook as agent of change. *English Language Teaching Journal*, 48(4), 315-328.

Lems, K. (1996). For a song: Music across the ESL curriculum. *Paper presented at the annual convention of Teachers of English to Speakers of Other Languages, Chicago.* (Ed. No. 396 524)

McDonough, J., & Shaw, C. (2003). *Materials and Methods in ELT.* Second Edition. Oxford: Blackwell.

McGrath, I. (2002). *Materials Evaluation and Design for Language Teaching.* Edinburgh: Edinburgh University Press.

Nunan, D. (1988). *Syllabus Design.* Oxford: Oxford University Press.

Prabhu, N. (1987). *Second Language Pedagogy.* Oxford: Oxford University Press.

Puhl, C. (1989). Up from under: English training on the mines. *Report on 1988 research project conducted at Gold Field Training Services.* Stellenbosch, South Africa: University of Stellenbosch. (Ed. No. 335 864)

Richards, J. (2001). *Curriculum Development in Language Teaching.* Cambridge: Cambridge University Press.

Sheldon, L. (Ed.) (1988). *ELT Textbooks and Materials: Problems in Evaluation and Development":* ELT Documents 126: Modern English Publications/The British Council.

Sheldon, L. (1988). Evaluating ELT textbooks and materials. *ELT Journal,* 42(4), 237-246.

Tomlinson, B. (1998). *Materials Development in Language Teaching.* Cambridge: Cambridge University Press.

Tomlinson, B. (2003). *Developing Materials for Language Teaching.* London: Continuum Press.

Tomlinson, B. (Ed.) (2008). *English Language Learning Materials: A Critical Review.* London: Continuum Press.

Walker, A. (1982). *The color purple: A novel.* New York, NY: Harcourt.

White, R. (1988). *The ELT Curriculum: Design, Innovation and Management,* Oxford: Basil Blackwell.

Wilkins, D. (1976) *Notional Syllabuses,* Oxford University Press.

INDEX

```
┌──────────────────────────────┐
│              O               │
└──────────────────────────────┘
```

```
┌──────────────────────────────┐
│              P               │
└──────────────────────────────┘
```

7104912R00130

Printed in Great Britain
by Amazon.co.uk, Ltd.,
Marston Gate.